SURVIVING
information overload

SURVIVING
information overload

The clear, practical

guide to help you

stay on top of what

you need to know

kevin a. miller

ZONDERVAN™

GRAND RAPIDS, MICHIGAN 49530 USA

We want to hear from you. Please send your comments about this
book to us in care of zreview@zondervan.com. Thank you.

ZONDERVAN™

Surviving Information Overload
Copyright © 2004 by Kevin A. Miller

This title is also available as a Zondervan ebook product. Visit
www.zondervan.com/ebooks for more information.

Requests for information should be addressed to:
Zondervan
Grand Rapids, Michigan 49530

Library of Congress Cataloging-in-Publication Data
Miller, Kevin A., 1960-
  Surviving information overload : the clear, practical guide to help you stay on top
of what you need to know / Kevin A. Miller.
    p. cm.
  Includes bibliographical references and index.
  ISBN 0-310-25115-X
  1. Information resources management.   2. Time management.   I. Title.
T58.64.M554 2004
020—dc22

2003027901

Interior design by Tracey Moran

Printed in the United States of America

---

05 06 07 08 /❖ DC/ 10 9 8 7 6 5 4 3

TO DAVE GOETZ, WHO TOLD ME,

"THERE'S A BOOK IN YOUR IDEAS."
"NO WAY," I SAID.

OKAY, YOU WERE RIGHT.

Contents

Part 3

CREATING SPACE TO THINK
Finding an oasis amid the overload

Part 4

BONUS STUFF
Hey, it doesn't cost you anything extra

1. **Take a deep breath.** Take another. There is a lot of fear today about not keeping up. But you're going to make it. You will learn how to surf the information tidal wave, and this book is going to help.
2. **You don't have to finish this book.** Read only as much as you find helpful. To help you find what you need, I've spelled out precisely what's in each chapter—both in the table of contents and at the start of each chapter.
3. **Feel free to skim read,** tear out pages, email small sections to a friend, or read from the back to the front. It doesn't matter if you read this book in the traditional way. It does matter that you come away with ideas and help.
4. To paraphrase author Fred Smith, **"This book is not about how to speed up.** People are already going fast enough. This book is about how to gain some time and focus and purpose and the mental space to be creative. I don't care if you loaf in your newfound time. In fact, you ought to use part of it for loafing. If you're already panicky, harried, frantic, and worn out from the pressure, don't spend your new time reading more emails, or you'll be right back in the same problem."[1]

part 1

FINDING

the Information You Need

And getting results from it

chapter 1

WHAT WE'RE UP AGAINST

Today's unprecedented problem:
too much information

Read this chapter if:

❑ You don't understand why you feel so overloaded; you didn't always feel that way.

❑ You keep expecting things to get less stressful, but that day doesn't seem to be coming.

❑ You want to read this book but don't feel you can spare the time.

You're normal. You're not crazy. But too much information may be making you feel stressed, distracted, or overwhelmed. Do you recognize any of the following signs of information overload?

1. You feel life has become just too complicated.
2. You know your cell phone, PDA, or laptop can do a whole lot more than you're using it for, but you don't have time to read the manual or help programs.

3. You miss a meeting and are upset that nobody told you about it. Then you find out you were sent an email that moved up the meeting date, but that email is still in your inbox, unread.
4. You attended a great seminar and took notes, but as soon as you got back, the crazy pace picked up again, and you haven't done anything with the notes yet.
5. Someone mentions a book you haven't read or a movie you haven't seen. You nod as if you have.
6. You find it nearly impossible to concentrate on a project because of phone calls, email, voice mail, and interruptions.
7. You go to vote, and you don't really know anything about most of the candidates on the ballot.
8. Your mind keeps churning after you go to bed and keeps you awake.
9. There was a time when you wanted the PC, digital camera, or DVD with the most features; now you just want the simplest.
10. You recently had an important file or check in your office, but for the life of you, you can't find it.
11. A country has been in the news a lot lately, but you're not exactly sure where that country is.
12. You have a stack of journals, magazines, and books that never seems to shrink.
13. You're starting to wonder if your memory is slipping, and you're writing things down more than ever because you can't keep it all in your head.
14. It seems like another person in the meeting understands what's going on, but you're not 100 percent sure you do.

15. You worry that your marketability is declining because your industry knowledge is getting out of date.[1]

If you recognized yourself in four or more of these statements, you're awash in information.

Maybe you feel like my friend Jim, who is the head of an association: "It's common for me to be working away on my computer, and I hear the little 'bing' that tells me another e-mail has arrived. While I'm looking at that new e-mail, which will take about a half hour to dispose of properly, another little 'bing' comes, and another, and another, until it sounds like my computer is a monotone xylophone. Then the phone rings, and the day's mail is stacked so high I can't even see my to-read pile of books on the corner of my desk. Stuff just keeps coming in faster than I can handle it, and I feel like Charlie Chaplin in *Modern Times*, when he's tightening screws on a production line and stops to scratch his head, getting hopelessly behind."[2]

We need information just to be able to shop, vote, earn money, and use our phone, but the information keeps coming—more and more, faster and faster—until we become frustrated, confused, and unsure of ourselves. Richard Saul Wurman writes that today we feel "a pervasive fear that we are about to be overwhelmed by the very material we need to master in order to function in this world."[3]

Why do we feel overloaded by information? What is going on?

Let me explain five forces unique to our time.

♣ *The world is now producing nearly two exabytes of new and unique information per year.*[4] Don't feel bad if you don't know what an exabyte is. No one does. It's a new term, one they had to coin for a billion gigabytes. The bottom line: more new information has been produced in the last 30 years than in the last 5,000.[5] Or to say it even more simply, "A weekday edition of the *New York Times* contains more information than the average person was likely to come across in a lifetime in seventeenth-century England."[6]

♣ *New communications technology exposes us to more ideas than ever before.* In *Playing the Future*, Douglas Rushkoff explains, "Inventions like the telephone, radio, television, photocopier, fax machine, modem, cable TV, video teleconferencing, computer bulletin board, and the World Wide Web all function to increase the number of people whose thoughts we encounter. Each successive development in communications technology—whether it's a cellular phone or an e-mail account—brings a corresponding leap in the number of ideas we're forced to process."[7]

♣ *Work has moved from the floor of the factory to the inside of our heads.* "Ideas are the new steel," writes Melinda Davis in *The New Culture of Desire.* "This transition from a manufacturing-driven economy to an idea-driven one has ... relocated great numbers of workers to a new Cerebral-Industrial Complex inside our own heads. At the beginning of the twentieth century, two-thirds of working Americans earned their living by making things, Henry Ford style. At the beginning of the twenty-first century, two-thirds earn a living by making decisions."[8]

This shift means, as David Brooks explains in *Newsweek*, that "today's business people live in an overcommunicated world. There are too many Web sites, too many reports, too many bits of information bidding for their attention. The successful ones are forced to become deft machete wielders in this jungle of communication. They ruthlessly cut away at all the extraneous data that are encroaching upon them. They speed through their tasks so they can cover as much ground as possible, answering dozens of e-mails at a sitting and scrolling past dozens more. After all, the main scarcity in their life is not money; it's time. They guard every precious second, the way a desert wanderer guards his water."[9]

♣ *Most information we get is badly presented or incomprehensible.* Even the basics of our lives have become complex and forbidding. Humorist Dave Barry writes, "If you're wondering what a Keogh Plan is, the technical answer is: Beats me. All I know is, I have one, and the people who administer it are always sending me Important Tax Information. Here's the first sentence of their most recent letter, which I swear I am not making up: 'Dear David: The IRS has extended the deadline for the restatement of your plan to comply with GUST and various other amendments until, in most instances, September 30, 2003.' I understand everything in that sentence up to 'David.' After that I am lost."[10]

♣ *Information used to be held in check because it could reach us through only a few channels at a few set times. No longer.* It's hard to remember now, but news came via a newspaper, which was published only in the morning or the evening. TV news flickered on at 5:00 or 10:00 P.M. But the rest of the day, news hid; you couldn't find it. Now CNN, websites, news-tracker emails, and updates on your cell phone wiggle their way into your mind all day, every day. Then the entire zoo escapes: 260,000 billboards, 11,520 newspapers, 11,556 periodicals, 27,000 video outlets, 40,000 new book titles, and 60,000,000,000 pieces of junk mail every year.[11]

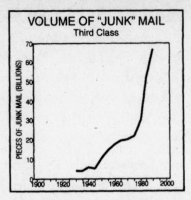

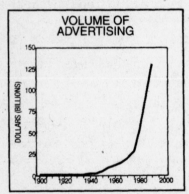

MORE DOESN'T WORK ANYMORE

You could engrave this on a plaque: MORE DOESN'T WORK ANYMORE.

In his fine book *Information Anxiety*, Richard Saul Wurman reminds us, "Since the advent of the industrial age, we have had a terrific word: 'More.' It really worked for everything. When our roads became crowded, we built more roads. When our cities became unsafe, we hired more police officers, ordered more police cars, and built more prisons." But when it comes to information, Wurman declares, "More doesn't work anymore."[12]

When the instruction book that comes with my cell phone runs 148 pages, more doesn't work anymore. When TV serves up 67 channels on cable and 128 on satellite, more doesn't work anymore. When a doctor has to read 250 articles every day to stay current, more doesn't work anymore.[13] When a daily paper contains 150,000 words, more doesn't work anymore.

Our weary little minds are huffing and puffing, trying to keep up, and they can't. Unlike computers, our brains don't operate on Moore's Law: our processing power doesn't double every eighteen months. G. K. Chesterton, the great British journalist, wrote, "Civilization has run on ahead of the soul of man, and is producing faster than he can think and give thanks." What scares me is that he wrote that in 1902—before voice mail, email, and the web. If civilization used to run on ahead, it now takes a jet.

More information than we can handle makes us feel disturbing feelings. See if you relate to any of the following symptoms.

♣ *Overloaded*. Vicki, the vice president of Internet operations for a publishing company, told me about when she began managing the department: "I was supposed to be leading an area about which I knew very little. I felt overloaded and overwhelmed by the amount of information out there—and by my inability to locate, evaluate, and integrate it quickly enough. I needed to know everything yesterday."

Or maybe you relate to Alan, a normally upbeat pastor and writer, who sighed when he told me, "Even books for dummies run 200 or 300 pages long! Give me 20 or 30."

A recent college graduate complains, "I read the *New York Times*, which contains a book review, which gives me another book to read. The more I read, the more I find there is to understand."

No wonder the fastest-growing magazine in America is *Real Simple*. Its circulation hit 1.2 million recently. Managing editor Carrie Tuhy explains why: "People have so many choices. The world has gotten so much more complicated. People need someone to be their personal navigator."[14]

♣ *Distracted*. Can't concentrate in your office? Maybe it's because "the average office worker receives some 220 messages a day in multiple media."[15] In *The New Culture of Desire*, Melinda Davis explains: "The world attacks us with a constant assault of stimulation and distraction, assigns us more tasks than a regiment of wizards could ever finish, and forces us to multitask—to 'semi-attend' to everything. *Wired* magazine calls ADD the 'official brain syndrome of the Information Age.'"[16]

♣ *Guilty*. Many people feel guilt over not being better informed. Said one executive, "I carry a great deal of guilt at times over what I am not reading and don't know. Because information is so readily available, there is a nagging sense of failure that I am not intelligent enough to absorb and apply more of it. I've set up systems, but they have not assuaged the guilt, the nagging sense that I could find a few more hours and use them well."

♣ *Frustrated*. While we get plenty of information—too much— is it any good? When ethnic wars broke out in Bosnia, news anchors told me how many people got killed in each day's shelling. They showed thirty-second clips of damaged homes.

But the underlying meaning remained murky. Who were these Bosnians, Serbians, Croatians? Which were Muslims and which were Catholics? Why were they really fighting? Where is Montenegro, and how does it connect? I was getting plenty of information, but I couldn't make sense of it all.

Richard Saul Wurman writes, "The opportunity is that there is so much information; the catastrophe is that 99 percent of it isn't meaningful or understandable."[17] Maybe you've tried to read the manual on how to operate your digital camera, and you can't quite figure it out. You don't know exactly what a megapixel is or why you would want more of them. The manual is thick, but it doesn't really explain your questions. That leads to a common, frustrating feeling: *The more I read, the less I understand.*

♣ *Half sick.* Professor John Killinger recalls "a Vanderbilt graduate student who came to me for counseling because she was having peculiar experiences. She would go into the library and become so overwhelmed by all of the books and all she needed to learn to get her master's degree in history that she had the impression the books on the shelves were all chattering at the same time. She had to get out of the library, out to where it was calm and peaceful again."[18]

Believe it or not, too much information, coming too fast, can make us sick. Melinda Davis, founder and CEO of the Next Group, points out, "We have to deal with an amazing internal commotion: competing, disembodied voices, all battling for top-of-the-mind attention; a constant blitz of stimulation; the grinding gears of brain exertion; relentless, after-hours brain spinning. . . . More than half of American adults . . . say that their brains continue to churn at night when they should be sleeping. . . . The Centers for Disease

Control and Prevention state unequivocally that 80 percent of our medical expenditures are now stress related."[19]

Still not convinced that information can make you sick? A survey of 1,313 managers on four continents found that "one-third of managers suffer from ill health, as a direct consequence of stress associated with information overload. This figure increases to 43 percent among senior managers."[20]

In *Too Loud, Too Bright, Too Fast, Too Tight*, developmental psychologist Sharon Heller argues that in today's hyperstimulated world, perhaps up to 15 percent of adults suffer from some form of "sensory defensiveness."[21] Writes Jeffrey Kluger, who reviewed Heller's book for *Time:* "Maybe you stick a Post-It note over your blinking e-mail icon because the flashing distracts you. Maybe you run an air conditioner in November to drown out the sound of a car alarm that doesn't seem to bother anyone else." The coping soon becomes its own problem; your daily decisions are driven by trying to protect yourself from too much stimulation.[22]

I HAVE GOOD NEWS FOR YOU

The promise of this book is that despite information overload, you can learn to live and lead with focus, purpose, and results. When the tidal wave of paper and email rolls in, you can learn to surf.

In my approach, you don't have to be relentlessly organized. You don't have to buy a bulky system of binders or a bloated software program or a color-coded anything. Most people don't need neatness; they need a new strategy.

I want to give you the essential skills that will allow you to recognize the information you need and to get results from that information. The simple but powerful strategies I present in this book have been proven. They've been tested in publishing companies and marketing companies, in businesses, associations, and churches, in large organizations and sole proprietorships. These strategies have made a huge difference in my life and in the lives of people who've learned them.

You may have only enough time to read portions of this book. You may be so stressed and overloaded that you can apply only a fraction of what you read. Even so, I predict that as you put to work even small amounts of what's in this book, you'll notice the difference. You'll get behind less and not feel as overwhelmed. You'll make better decisions because you'll have the information you need. You'll find yourself growing, learning, and accomplishing more than you were before.

After reading only parts of three chapters in this book, one man wrote me, "I used to get so discouraged at not finishing some of the books on my shelf. Also [I felt] being overwhelmed at times trying to keep up with the minutes of meetings ... But now I am learning to just do a list of action notes to be followed up on. The idea of applying at least one thing from what I read, learn or experience has [meant that handling information has] gone from a frustrating exercise to an attainable goal."[23]

You don't have to drown; you can learn to swim.

Let me quickly orient you to this book so you can decide which sections will be most helpful to you. The book has three main parts, plus a bonus part.

Part 1, "Finding the Information You Need," answers the question, "What do I *do* with all this information coming at me?" This section helps you select your key information areas (chapter 2), capture the information you need (chapter 3), and get results from that information (chapter 4). Chapter 4 covers one of the least talked about but most important skills for our time.

Part 2, "Clearing Information Clutter," helps you reduce the flow of incoming email, voice mail, and junk mail. The strategies presented in these chapters (5–9) will lower your stacks of books, magazines, and newspapers. And they will help you find what you need, both in your office and on the Internet. Pick the chapters that apply to you.

Part 3, "Creating Space to Think," helps you find an oasis amid the overload so you can quiet your soul, think, and create again. Don't miss chapter 12, "Why We Secretly Like Overload," because it speaks to our motivations, and when we address our real motivations, we can see lasting, positive change. I'm also fond of chapter 13, "Blessed Are They Who Admit Their Ignorance . . . ," a counterintuitive whack on the side of the head.

Part 4, "Bonus Stuff," is like the extra features on a DVD: check them out or skip them.

I hope you'll explore this book, that you'll read at least parts of it and apply some of the ideas to your life, because it will help you move from having too much information to having the right information. It will help you turn intention into action. It will help you live and lead with wisdom.

As you read, you may have questions, suggestions, or additional ideas. If so, I'd like to hear from you. Send me an email at kmiller@mailcti.com.

QUESTIONS TO APPLY

- In my life right now, what symptoms of information overload do I feel?

- On a scale from 1 (low) to 5 (high), how ready am I to read and apply solutions to the problem of information overload?

QUOTES TO TAKE WITH YOU

" We are like a thirsty person who has been condemned to use a thimble to drink from a fire hydrant.

—*Richard Saul Wurman*[24]

" Of making many books there is no end, and much study wearies the body.

—*Ecclesiastes 12:12*

chapter 2

SELECTING YOUR KEY INFORMATION AREAS

What must you know, and what can you safely ignore?

Read this chapter if:

❑ You'd love to not have to keep up with everything, but you don't know what you can safely ignore.

❑ You could use more focus in your learning.

Let me begin with a simple, wonderfully freeing premise: You do not need to know everything.

A few short generations ago, it could rightly be said, Information is power. That was true when there wasn't enough of it. Today the motto should read, Information is fatigue. We get too much information, and a high percentage of that information is inane, meaningless, and enervating. Do I really need to know whom Anne Heche is dating?

Writes Richard Saul Wurman, in *Information Anxiety 2*: "Information was once a sought-after and treasured commodity like a fine wine. Now, it's regarded more like crab-grass, something to be kept at bay."[1]

No, information alone is no longer power. What is power is the *right* information, a limited amount of information—the information you need, when you need it.

The fact that we must focus our learning should be self-evident, but for many years, I struggled to believe it. Growing up, I admired DaVinci, Benjamin Franklin, and other polymaths who excelled in multiple fields. I believed the gold crown of knowledge rested on those whose learning ranged across disciplines: Blaise Pascal, Desiderius Erasmus, Albert Schweitzer. I chose a liberal-arts college because I believed in being well-rounded.

But whatever understandable forces create the longing to be a Renaissance scholar, guess what? We aren't living in the Renaissance. In fact, as Richard Swenson says, "Francis Bacon, a contemporary of Shakespeare, is regarded by historians as the last person to know everything in the world. Since then, each of us learns a progressively smaller percentage of all the information that exists."[2]

You and I live during a time when the universe of knowledge has exploded—giant galaxies of learning are expanding and streaming apart. My favorite search engine, Google, currently indexes 3,307,998,701 web pages. My mind can't comprehend that number, let alone those pages' contents. And the number of web pages nearly tripled in eighteen months. I can't know everything.

This truth keeps me humble and dependent on others. It also frees me to concentrate my learning in key areas. I can always ask others about what I don't know, and no one should be afraid to do that. Ignorance is not a sin; acting like you know something when you don't is.

Ah, but here's the rub: How do you determine which areas of learning not to concentrate on? What information can you neglect with impunity?

A business executive told me he struggles with this dilemma: "I live in the general world of marketing, but there are multiple disciplines of marketing, including graphic design, print direct-mail marketing, email marketing, CRM software, marketing strategy, and more. I need to be an expert, but I can't be an expert in everything. How do I select which discipline to drill down in?"

Here's how: by answering the following five questions, you will develop your unique answer.

✓ *Is there someone else who is an expert on this topic—or could be?* If the answer is yes, then how knowledgeable do you really need to be in this area?

Sole proprietors or start-up entrepreneurs may need to be experts on copier repair or mailing permits, for no one else has the time or energy to be. But in general, if anyone else knows (or would enjoy finding out) the details, why should you?

My work, for example, involves overseeing five paid-content websites, so I need to know about changes in the online world. But I've decided I don't need to be an online savant; other staff members can be. I need only be conversant enough to ask them intelligent questions. This decision saves me hours of reading every month.

This distributed-knowledge approach has a price, however. It means I sometimes have to admit, "I don't know; ask So-and-so," which can be mildly embarrassing. But as Peter Drucker explains, "Once beyond the apprentice stage, knowledge workers must know more about their job than their boss does—or what good are they?"[3] This approach empowers my staff and colleagues: they are the experts, and I have to trust their knowledge.

One manager says, "I gradually learned the most effective strategy was to find out the knowledge level of my staff—and rely on all they knew in specific areas. By looking to my staff to be the experts, I reduced the clutter in my thinking and could focus on learning the things that only I was responsible for."

If someone else can be the expert on a particular topic, you probably don't need to make that your key learning area.

✓ *Can questions in this information area be looked up relatively quickly?* Have you heard the (possibly apocryphal) story of the student who asked Albert Einstein, "Dr. Einstein, how many feet are there in a mile?"

Einstein said he didn't know.

The student assumed he had to be joking, but when pressed for an explanation, Einstein answered, "I make it a rule not to clutter my mind with simple information that I can find in a book in five minutes."

Hey, if Einstein was right about the general theory of relativity, I figure he's probably right about this. Why study something that can be readily retrieved?

In my work, I am responsible for a sizable budget with multiple accounts. People expect me to know the budget. But the truth is, I don't really know it (except in broad terms), and I don't need to. I keep a thick, blue notebook with financial budgets and reports, and when someone asks me a question about the budget, I simply pull out the notebook.

You don't need to know it if you know where to look it up.

"Sorry, Doctor Jones won't be able to see you today.
He has paralysis of analysis."

✓ *Is this topic essential for decisions I'm making now or will be making in the near future?* Years ago I visited Leith Anderson, pastor of Wooddale Church near Minneapolis, when the church was building its current sanctuary. As we walked through the construction site, Leith pointed to one wall that would form the back of the sanctuary. "See that?" he asked. "We had to ask for special rubber sound-absorbing insulation on that wall, because there's a rest room on the opposite side, and we didn't want the sound of a flush to reverberate into the sanctuary during a quiet moment in worship."

Verily, I'd never thought of that.

Yet Leith knew the fine points of construction: whether the insulation needed to be a three-quarters or three-eighths of an inch, the relative advantages of large brick versus small brick, and the material costs per square foot. "I've learned what I've needed to as we've faced major decisions," he explained. "Before next month's board meeting, I'm going to learn everything I can about educational classrooms."

For Leith, minute knowledge of construction practices was necessary, but only for a limited time. Once the building was built, he could forget most of what he'd studied. The key principle: Learn what you need for the decisions you're making now.

✓ *What subjects do the most important people around me depend on me to know?* What does my boss (this may be a board, stockholders, or constituents) legitimately expect me to stay on top of?

Try to answer that question now. My boss rightly expects me to stay on top of: _____

_____

_____

_____

The problem is that we almost always list too many subjects when answering this question. Can you shorten your list?

An entrepreneur I know learned this lesson the hard way. She would work all day, raising capital, launching the business, dealing with cash flow. Then at night she would try to read a dozen business and trade publications. "I'd rip out the articles to read whenever I had the time," she says. "Problem was, I never seemed to have the time to get to all those articles, either."

The solution was to narrow the list of subjects she studied, to the precious few her investors depended on her to know: e-commerce and marketing. "It made more sense for me to focus on a finite area of the industry and leave the rest behind. Little by little, I stopped subscribing to the periodicals, especially the ones that stacked up faster than the rest. (It helped that some of those periodicals went out of business!)"

Yes, some topics you truly need to know, because people depend on you to know them. But that list is probably much smaller than you'd think.

✓ *Does this area fit my life's calling and my major strengths?*

Fred Smith, winner of the Lawrence Appley award for excellence in business, has taught, "When I know the ultimate purpose of my life, I can know whether I'm using my time properly. If I do not know that ultimate purpose, I have no way of judging my efficiency."[4]

I take that lesson to heart. I must first know the ultimate purpose of my life. Only then can I determine where to invest my learning time. I should learn the areas of knowledge that help express the ultimate purpose of my life. I should study in my areas of strength. This sounds self-evident, but I find people generally disregard the idea.

Why? Here are some of the reasons I hear:

- "I feel my weaknesses more acutely; I need to shore up those."
- "My strengths come naturally to me, so I don't need to study in those areas."
- "I feel guilty just reading about what I enjoy."

I understand these reasons. I've even read a book on information overload that manages only eleven pages before it advocates you list areas of "self-improvement: what I am not very good at and need/want to improve."

I disagree with this approach. In my opinion, life is too short for me to be constantly shoring up my weaknesses. I'll never fix them all. How much more productive to recognize and build on my strengths. Thus, I choose my learning areas largely by focusing on my gifts—areas of talent or strength.

According to several assessment tools, my primary strengths are teaching, wisdom, and leadership. So I read regularly and without apology about teaching, decision making, and leadership. I study books with titles like *Biblical Preaching* or *Courageous Leadership*. I want to do better what I'm supposed to be doing with my life.

Why should I select as a key learning area something in which I can, at best, be only pretty good? You can teach a dog to ride a pony, but it will never win a rodeo. Ben Patterson, an author I like, puts it this way: "I would rather know a few things well than a lot of things pretty well. I'm told this happens when we get older. I'm more accepting of what my genuine interests and strengths are, and I'm going with those."[5]

So my advice is to pretty much ignore your weaknesses and study in your areas of strength. If you do this, you will learn faster and enjoy it more. Richard Saul Wurman explains that before learning can take place, there must be interest. "You can't get lost on the road to interest."[6]

CREATING YOUR SHORT LIST

Now you're ready to list your key areas for study, using the table on page 34. This will be a rough draft; feel free to erase or scratch out as you go. For each area of study, make sure it fits most or all of the five criteria we have discussed:

1. No one else on my team or in my life can be the expert on this topic; it's something only I can specialize in.

2. This area of information can't readily be looked up or obtained elsewhere.
3. This is a topic on which I'm making major decisions now or in the near future.
4. The most important people in my work or life depend on me to know this topic.
5. This topic fits my life's calling and my strengths.

MY KEY INFORMATION AREAS

If you're like me, you will end up with a short list, a modest list, a manageable list. Your goal is to eliminate enough topics so you can concentrate deeply on others. Eliminate and concentrate.[7]

Yes, you will lose knowledge of some things, which stings. I got an email from a man who described himself as "a Renaissance person: certificated educator, published composer, ordained minister, published author, Ph.D. professor, somewhat-effective executive, radio speaker, parachurch ministry leader, husband and father." He admitted, "It's hard to resist diversified learning, since life is so interesting!"[8]

I feel the same way. But the alternative to a short list is not more learning, but less effectiveness. Let T. D. Jakes describe what happens to the person who refuses to set priorities: "Overloaded people fail. They always have and they always will. . . . Like an airplane, we can only carry a certain amount of weight. If we have too much baggage on board, we will be ineffective and we won't be able to soar. Most people end up exceeding the weight limit. Motivated by the desire to please, impress, or otherwise gain commendation, they take on too much and, in the end, fail to reach the heights of success or else crash because they ignored their limitations.

"In order to maximize your life, you have to minimize your load."[9]

By the way, your short list will change over time, and that's fine and necessary. Twenty years ago, when I edited curriculum for youth groups, my list read like this: youth work, adolescent development, educational approaches, and writing. I stayed up to date on the trends, key thinkers, and important developments in these areas. Now I ignore most information on youth work or education, not because those subjects are unimportant but because they're not my current areas of learning.

Today my list reads: paid-content online, leadership, new product development, and preaching. Notice the vast realms of knowledge not on my list. For example, I don't study writing in depth as I once did. But at this stage of my life, writing is not the information area I need to study most.

Final check: If your list holds more than five key information areas, you probably are still not giving up enough. Remember the powerful premise of this chapter: You do not need to know everything. Less is more.

Refuse to be pulled out of your key areas by insecurity over what other people know—or claim they know. Alan Nelson, who pastors a church in Scottsdale, says, "It's easy to get intimidated by leaders who tell you about twelve books they've just read. But I have to ask, 'If I were to read those books, how would I really benefit? How would my people benefit? What good comes of it?'"[10]

CAVE ART

Okay, okay, now that I've insisted you can't list more than five learning areas at a time, I'm going to open a loophole. A big loophole.

Everything I've said so far assumes you want greater focus and effectiveness in your work. But that's not the only reason we learn, nor the most important reason we learn. We also read to escape, to meditate and reflect, to recalibrate our lives, to grow spiritually, to enjoy learning.

I think of those early humans, 17,000 years ago, who speared mammoths and painted on cave walls in southern France. They were masters of hunting and masters of art. Some of the time, probably most of the time, they focused on hunting, stalking bison and ibex, spearing their game, just trying to eat in order to live another day. But they felt another impulse, to create something of beauty, to pick up a piece of charcoal or iron and sketch large red cows, a herd of yellow horses running wild, a fierce black bull with massive forelegs and curved horns sharpening to a point. What possible benefit did they derive from painting the walls of their cave? Paintings didn't fill their stomach or warm their body or protect their family. But as humans, they needed to paint, and today we know about them and care about them because they did.

Similarly, there is a focused study for everyday effective-ness—the reading of the Hunt. Just as essential to life is a meditative, meandering, muse-led study for the expression and expansion of our soul—the reading of the Cave Art.

Your learning list should include Cave Art areas, subjects that seemingly offer no immediate practical benefit, that stimulate your imagination, broaden your understanding, and deepen your empathy. Listen to some people describe their Cave Art areas of learning:

> *Jay Kesler:* "I read novels for enjoyment, escape, and enrichment. I read John LeCarre spy novels for the intrigue. I read and reread authors like Dostoyevsky, Tolstoy, Chekhov because I cannot have every human experience, and . . . good novels let us live life in ways we can't otherwise. You can learn more about the soul, for example, the plight of the sinner caught in systemic sin, by reading Dostoyevsky than by almost any other way.[11]
>
> *David Hansen:* "I mostly read dead people. Reading things that are old delivers me from the feeling of information overload. So much of what's promoted now will be gone in three or four years."[12]
>
> *Fred Smith:* "I want to stay close to certain writers, even though I already know what they have to say. I read Oswald Chambers, for example, nearly every day. I want to maintain a personal relationship with his type of thinking, his personality."[13]

If you had to list Cave Art areas you would love to study now, what would those be? Add one or two of these topics to the list you made on page 34.

I find that my Cave Art areas change more frequently than my Hunt areas. I flit and float, like a butterfly crossing a meadow and landing on different flowers: history, modern politics, murder mysteries, race relations in America. For two or three years I read spiritual classics of the Christian West—Jonathan Edwards' *Religious Affections*, Martin Luther's *Commentary on Galatians*; Benedict's *Rule*. (Uh, I also read *Zits* comic books.)

Further—and this is profoundly important—when studying Cave Art topics, I read in a different way. Sven Birkerts calls it deep reading, or vertical reading. But for me, its best description comes from Eugene Peterson, who calls it spiritual reading: "Spiritual reading is mostly a lover's activity—a dalliance with words, reading as much between the lines as in the lines themselves. It is leisurely, as ready to reread an old book as to open a new one. It is playful, anticipating the pleasures of friendship. It is prayerful, convinced that all honest words can involve us in some way, if we read with our hearts as well as our heads. . . . Spiritual reading, for most of us, requires either the recovery or acquisition of skills not in current repute: leisurely, repetitive, reflective reading. In this we are not reading primarily for information, but for companionship. . . . It is a way of reading that shapes the heart at the same time that it informs the intellect, sucking out the marrow-nourishment from the bone-words. . . ."[14]

By now you should have selected a short list of your key areas of information, the topics of study that will focus your learning. That list includes areas of the Hunt, topics that have immediate application to your daily life, and areas of Cave Art, topics that nourish your soul. Happy hunting. Happy painting.

QUESTIONS TO APPLY

- Am I truly interested in each topic I listed? Or did I list something I'm not truly interested in? If so, what caused me to list that topic?

- Which am I more likely to lose from my life: the reading of the Hunt or the reading of the Cave Art?

QUOTES TO TAKE WITH YOU

" Each should know what he ought to read; second, in what order he ought to read; and third, in what manner he ought to read.
> —*Hugh of St. Victor (writing in the twelfth century)*

" Before I tell my life what I want to do with it, I must listen to my life telling me who I am.
> —*Parker Palmer*[15]

chapter 3

THE FINE ART OF CAPTURING GOOD IDEAS

How to retain the information you really need

Read this chapter if:

❑ You have good ideas and can't remember them later.

❑ You're not sure how best to gather information when you're working on a project.

John Kilcullen was eating dinner with a friend. This friend described overhearing someone ask a bookstore clerk, "Do you have any simple books on Microsoft DOS—something like *DOS for Dummies?*"

That throwaway comment—a joke—stuck with Kilcullen, and he launched the *For Dummies* books, now a worldwide phenomenon, selling more than 100 million copies, in 39 languages.[1] "So often you hear an idea and you forget it," says Kilcullen in the *Marketing Revolution Newsletter.* "Or you hear an idea, you write it down, but you don't act upon it. Grab the idea, write it down and do something with it."[2]

To survive information overload, it's critical to capture the good ideas you have or hear or read. Building a healthy storage-and-retrieval system lightens the load of too much information. Why? It saves you the frustration of losing an idea. It saves you the time and work of rummaging for the idea later or starting a search from scratch. By preserving the idea, you can do something with it.

Don't underestimate the power of immediately capturing a good idea. My friend Dave, founder of CustomZines.com, says, "The more time that passes from when the idea hits me, the less heat it gives off. I forget parts of it, it doesn't seem as great. But the idea is great. The problem is that ideas have a short half-life. For example, I'm still trying to work on a book I started two years ago, but I can't, because I'm not capturing my observations for that topic. I'm still receiving good ideas, but I'm not recording them."[3]

PURPOSE-DRIVEN LEARNING

I began the last chapter with a simple, wonderfully freeing premise: You do not need to know everything. You can select your key areas for learning. By limiting yourself to a short list of strategic learning areas, you save hours every week. You become gloriously free to ignore much of the information around you. You're unshackled from the stack of nonessential magazines, from major sections of the two-inch-thick Sunday paper, from half the email newsletters in your inbox. Focus sets you free.

In this chapter, I will show you how to strategically reinvest some of those hours you save.

Now that you know your key information areas, capture information related to those areas. No, you don't need most of the information coming at you, but you must focus on the information you do need. Your learning then becomes strategic, intentional, purpose driven. You record the ideas you hear or read or think—if they fall in your key areas of learning.

I've noticed a subtle but key difference between people who get things done and people who don't. We're all awash in information, but some leaders swim while others sink. The difference, I now know, lies in an essential skill: the skill of selecting the information most needed and holding on to that information. To keep from drowning in a heaving sea of information, you need to spot the strong floating timbers, swim to them, and hang on with all your strength.

I've dubbed this skill "capture." It's a simple discipline that will help you find and keep the ideas you need most.

CAPTURING YOUR BEST IDEAS

To capture my mental activity, I keep notepads in my car and on the nightstand in my bedroom. These are the transition points, the places in which I move from work to home or from rest to sleep. Ideas usually come out to play during the recesses of my day, and I don't want to miss them. Many ideas are mundane ("Don't forget to call Keith"), but some are profound ("Fénelon writes that in the spiritual life, to be embarrassed by your faults may be more of a problem than the faults themselves"). And even the mundane ideas matter; Keith feels good when I call him, which I wouldn't have done if I hadn't captured the idea.

Sure, some captured ideas I never use. That doesn't deter me. I have seen the tremendous power of capturing a good idea.

The way you gather information will vary from crayon-on-napkin to Pocket PC. In *Bird by Bird*, author Anne Lamott explains, "I have index cards and pens all over the house—by the bed, in the bathroom, in the kitchen, by the phones, and I have them in the glove compartment of my car. I carry one with me in my back pocket when I take my dog for a walk. In fact, I carry it folded lengthwise, if you need to know, so that, God forbid, I won't look bulky."

Why?

Lamott gives the answer: "I used to think that if something was important enough, I'd remember it until I got home, where I could simply write it down in my notebook like some normal functioning member of society. But then I wouldn't. . . . If it feels natural, if it helps you to remember, take notes. It's not cheating. It doesn't say anything about your character."[4]

My friend Dennis, one of the most extraordinary networkers I've met, carries a pocket-size dictating recorder. In the midst of lunch, he'll pull it out and record a brief message: "Call John to find out the questions he uses with search committees."

The key is to find a system, any system, that allows you to capture the ideas you need. One guy dedicates a section of his Day-Timer for ideas. A popular speaker uses numbered file folders. An artist I know carries a hardbound sketchbook with blank pages. Another friend of mine, a brilliant consultant, is writing a book on leadership. To capture ideas for his book, he's been jotting notes on the back of scrap 8-1/2-by-11-inch paper and putting the pages in a recycled three-ring binder. "That allows me to move around the pages later," he explains.

In *Fast Company*, Tom Peters writes that "Karl Weick, the brilliant University of Michigan professor of organizational behavior and psychology, has his own system: His sport coat doubles as a filing cabinet. He fills the pockets with anything that he can make notes on—scraps of paper, napkins, matchbook covers. Then, once a week, he empties out his tweed filing cabinet and records his observations."[5]

One CEO I know carries a journal with a brown leather cover and blank pages. One morning at breakfast I asked him about it. "I write in thoughts I have, as well as to-do lists," he explained. "I also write great phrases or stories from articles I've read. The real genius lies in those ideas that come to you during the day or in the midst of a conversation or in the middle of the night. Those get lost forever if they are not written down.

"I find those ideas don't come in a stream of consciousness but in cryptic phrases. That's why, if you don't write them down, you'll never see them again."

I asked him, "Give me an example."

He opened the leather-bound journal and began reading, "'The most important part of learning is how to unlearn errors.' I needed to write that down and think about it. Or listen to this: 'Wisdom is the reward of a lifetime of listening when you would have rather been talking.' That's from Aristotle."

I had to admit his journal led to deeper thought and more lasting learning.

"I now keep this journal by my side all day," he said. "It's not a thing of beauty. I don't want it to be a thing of beauty. But I've done some of my best thinking in this book. I love keeping it in my hands at all times."

We all receive too much information; those who survive capture a few good ideas and put them into a form they can use later. As one consultant explained, "Too many people are trying to do this bare-handed. Encourage them to find and start using a tool, and then the process of capture won't seem so difficult anymore."

TOO TIRING?

At this point, you may still be feeling, *This sounds tiring. I can't be on mental alert all the time.*

True, but you don't have to be.

Although you need to be more attentive to some things, you can be less attentive to many other things. For example, you may be reading a book right now and are struggling to finish it. Ask yourself, "If I'm not getting something out of this book—if this is not helping me in my key learning areas— why am I reading it?" You might save hours by not reading a book of marginal value. This more than offsets the minutes spent jotting notes from a book that is central to your growth.

In addition, your goal is to capture the information, but that doesn't mean you need to do all the capturing. I know several leaders who merely stick a Post-it note on a book page; from there, a secretary or volunteer creates a computer file or database entry.

Nor does capturing the information in a book or an article mean you even need to read it right now. Leith Anderson, pastor of a large church near Minneapolis, explains: "I set my preaching schedule a year in advance. I have a file folder for every sermon in the coming year. If I'm speaking on grief, for example, when I see an article on the subject, I'll tear it out and put it in the folder, usually without reading it. Then when I begin preparing for that sermon, I read the file."[6]

You may not even need to formally file the ideas you capture. Three fine leaders and thinkers I know don't use a filing system; they just keep a pile of cards or a journal, and periodically they reread what they've written, pulling out what they need at the moment. In the process of reading and reviewing their notes, they reinforce the ideas in their minds. One says, "This doesn't take much time; after a few weeks, a card is so familiar that one glance reminds me of its content."

Whatever system you design, the point is to gather—to record so you can use—the key ideas you need most.

GETTING THE PAYOFF

If you start to capture ideas, you'll be glad you did. That information will often pay off later, like a bond that reaches maturity. Here are some examples of how the simple practice of capturing ideas can help you.

From a book: I listened to an audio book about the Battle of Agincourt, one of the most surprising, lopsided military victories of all time and the basis of Shakespeare's *Henry V*. I chose the book because the Kenneth Branagh film *Henry V* had made me curious. I listened to this book purely for fun; it would be hard to imagine a topic that has less direct application to my life than a fifteenth-century battle fought with crossbows. Still, as I drove and listened to the book, I jotted ideas on note cards (trying hard not to cause an accident as I did). Then I typed those notes into a file on my laptop. It seemed like wasted time and energy.

A year later, though, I was asked to write an article on leadership for an email newsletter. My well of ideas came up dry. Then I remembered that Henry V had displayed amazing leadership of his troops. I found the file where I had jotted notes, double-clicked, and discovered everything I needed to write "Lessons in Leadership from King Henry V: What a Battle 600 Years Ago Can Teach Us Today."

From a seminar: I attended a conference titled "Accounting Principles for Non-Financial Managers." I thought it would help me, but I soon discovered that none of the ideas presented applied. I had signed up for the wrong seminar. But I was determined to capture something of value to me. So when I got back from the conference, I called my company's chief financial officer and said, "At this seminar, I learned that the main difference between cash and accrual accounting is this . . . Is that how you understand it? Which do we use here? Why?"

I discovered, which I hadn't known, that our company uses both methods—cash accounting, to track cash flow for day-to-day decisions, and accrual accounting, because that method is preferred by accountants. I learned something important about my company, which I would not have if I hadn't tried to capture one lesson, any lesson, from an ill-chosen seminar.

From a walk or random encounter: Novelist Anne Lamott writes, "Sometimes, if I overhear or think of an exact line of dialogue or a transition, I write it down verbatim. I stick the card back in my pocket. I might be walking along the salt marsh, or out at Phoenix Lake, or in the express line at Safeway, and suddenly I hear something wonderful that makes me want to smile or snap my fingers—as if it has just come back to me—and I take out my index card and scribble it down."[7]

From a meeting: In a meeting out of the office, I realized that someone in the room, a man named Dan, could help with another project at my company. I pulled out my laptop and typed a quick email to the people in charge of that project, recommending Dan. I might have remembered till I got back to the office, but probably not. And the recipients of the email thanked me and will probably act on the recommendation.

From a magazine article: I read a book review of Eugene Lowry's *The Sermon* and liked Lowry's structure for narratives: Conflict, Complication, Sudden Shift, Unfolding. I typed those words into a computer file, one that I often read when I prepare a sermon. The next time I preach a narrative message, I'll try to use that fourfold structure.

"Perhaps we shouldn't disturb him.
He seems to be deep in thought."

VECTORING IDEAS

As that last example indicates, not every idea you capture will be acted on immediately. That's fine. Some ideas you'll use in your next meeting, but other ideas—often the simplest and most powerful—should be stored away. A friend calls these ideas "vectoring ideas": Nothing changes at first, but over time, the idea re-vectors your life or your thought.

For example, for four or five years, I've been returning to this quotation from Fénelon: "Your mind is a good thing, but learn to distrust it and you will make better use of it." Gradually this idea I captured in my journal is re-vectoring me from overuse of the rational faculties toward a fuller use of my intuitive and spiritual capacities. I captured that idea, and now that idea has captured me.

Whenever or however an idea makes its impact, though, the process begins when you capture it. You must capture it first.

Several years ago, I asked Fred Smith, contributing editor for *Leadership* journal, to write a book for a new book series. Fred was in his eighties, so as his editor, I suggested he draw heavily from the vault of articles and books he had written over the years. The material was useful and hadn't lost its currency. I figured he could add one or two new chapters, and the book would be done.

Fred refused. "I want to write a new book," he said.

He had been reading extensively from the great spiritual writers like Molinos and Merton, and he was more concerned than ever about the leader's soul. So Fred started writing a book that went far beyond his extensive knowledge of business skills, into seasoned reflections on character and integrity in leadership.

I visited Fred to talk about the book, and we sat at his dining-room table. He pulled out several manila folders, each two inches thick and bulging with clippings, notes, articles, and jottings. Most were insights he had dictated and his assistant

Margie had later transcribed. No thoughts had been wasted or lost, no quotations were read and forgotten, but all had been captured so they could now be considered. No wonder he wanted to write a fresh book: he had a large bank account of captured ideas, and he merely needed to make a withdrawal.

The best of those captured insights were published in *Leading with Integrity*. In my opinion, it is Fred's finest book and will remain so—unless in his nineties he writes another.

QUESTIONS TO APPLY

- When in my day or week do I most often get fresh ideas? Where am I then?

- What would be the best way for me to capture ideas and information—notebook, PDA, or something else?

- Is there any way that someone else could help me gather the information and ideas I need?

QUOTES TO TAKE WITH YOU

" Study is not an alternative to experience but is itself a form of experience that grants understanding, even expertise, on a range of subjects.

—*Fred Craddock*

" I use not only all the brains I have, but all I can borrow.

—*Woodrow Wilson*

chapter 4

HOW TO TURN INFORMATION INTO RESULTS

You can put ideas to work for you

Read this chapter if:

- ❑ You're tired of meetings that go pretty well but then nothing happens afterward.

- ❑ You have a notebook from a seminar you attended but haven't had time to go through it.

- ❑ Somebody gave you a book and said, "You really ought to read this," but you don't have time.

Now we reach the most important chapter so far.

True wisdom does not come from information alone. Clifford Stoll quips that "data is not information any more than 50 tons of cement is a skyscraper."[1]

Wisdom comes from meditating on, then *acting* on, meaningful information. The biblical writer James exhorts us, "Do not merely listen to the word, and so deceive yourselves. Do what it says" (James 1:22). In a similar way, I can hear or read words and deceive myself into thinking I now know them. But I usually don't, not until I act on them. Writes Peter Drucker in *The Effective Executive*, "The greatest wisdom not applied to action and behavior is meaningless data."[2]

Let's look at the most common sources of information—seminars, meetings, books, and reports—to see how you can transform data into wisdom and turn information into results.

SEMINARS

Two people go to a seminar. Attendee A takes clear and accurate notes, which he puts in a notebook and files once he gets home. Attendee B scribbles only seven words on a napkin but makes specific changes in her work routine when she gets home.

Which person got the most out of the conference?

Not the person who took the most notes, but the one who applied a few ideas. The goal is not to take lots of notes—a good tape recorder can do that—but to improve the way you work. In fact, if an organization is paying for me to go to a seminar, I have an ethical responsibility to deliver a return on that investment. The only return I can make is to do my work $279 or $495 better than I did before the seminar. To do that, I must apply at least one thing I learned.

Over the years, I've developed several strategies that help me act on the information from seminars and conferences.

() Before I register, I ask myself, *Kevin, why do you want to go to this seminar—really?* Sometimes the answer is, *Because I want a break and need to get out of the office.* But if I need rest, I should rest and take a vacation day. If I attend a seminar, it should be because I want to learn. Now I check myself: If I register, am I willing to focus and to act on what I learn?

◌ At the seminar or conference, I take few notes. (This is a change: I used to scribble notes feverishly, until I realized, *I bring home all these notes, put them on my shelf, and never look at them again.*) But as I take my sparing notes, I draw a star next to any point I want to implement. What will I do, whom will I call, what will I change when I get back? I almost demand that the seminar will yield something useful, and when I find that useful idea, I draw a star.

For example, in a seminar on project management, I drew stars next to the following notes:

★ Tell Dave to hold off on ordering Microsoft Project. The seminar leader says that software becomes valuable when a project has more than fifty steps, and most of our projects run from twenty to forty steps long. (Taking action on this one item saved us the cost of the software, which was higher than the price of the seminar.)

★ When making a decision about a project, ask ourselves, "Which is most important: speed, quality, or cost?" (I wrote on a small card, "Speed, Quality, Cost," and hung it above my desk. After a few months, I routinely asked, "For this project, which is most important—speed, quality, or cost?" and I no longer needed to look at my card. The idea had been turned into action. The result: I made decisions faster and with more confidence.)

★ Get customer feedback as early in the project's lifespan as possible. We normally create a nearly perfect prototype and then talk to customers. But it would be more valuable to talk to customers as soon as we get the rough idea. (We started doing informal customer research early in the project, which saved us time spent on prototypes and money spent on focus groups.)

I drew only two or three other stars, even though the seminar lasted all day. The speaker spoke hundreds of thousands of words, which I did not record and do not remember. But I don't care, because I had selected five or six key ideas that applied to my work. Each of these ideas, because it was acted on, made me more effective. I'd have been happy with even one or two ideas acted on, and this seminar happened to give me five or six.

Remember: It's not how many notes you take, but how many ideas you act on.

() When I sign up for a seminar, I open my calendar and block a chunk of time on the day I will return. That's always a busy day, catching up on voice mail and email from when I was gone. But I try to fence off two hours in which I can look over my starred items and send memos, hold conversations, make calls, change systems. If I don't immediately act on the seminar's key ideas, I usually lose the motivation and then the insight. Alfred North Whitehead wrote, "Ideas won't keep. Something must be done about them. When the idea is new, its custodians have fervor, live for it, and, if need be, die for it."[3]

() I share what I learned with others. On my team of ten people, whenever one of us attends a seminar, that person reports to the group. At our next team meeting, the person takes fifteen minutes to describe the seminar highlights that most apply to our work. When we started this practice, I feared, *People won't want to hear about other people's seminars, or, It will create jealousy: not only did the person get to miss work for a day, but now he or she gets the spotlight in a meeting.* But those fears proved baseless. Several team members have told me they like the reports and learn from them. The most important result: Whenever someone attends a seminar, she goes into it thinking, *What can I find that's useful? I'm going to have to report on this.* She learns and applies more ideas, and that benefits nine other people.

MEETINGS

One important source of information for leaders is meetings. But how many times have you been in a committee meeting that went well, but in the weeks that followed, little or nothing happened? People either didn't remember or didn't act on what was said. So much talk, so little action.

Having endured this many times, I finally abandoned the traditional minutes of the meeting. Instead, I record a short, simple list of action steps. The only written record of the meeting lists what action will be taken, by whom, and when. Then I send this list to each person immediately after the meeting. For example:

WHO	ACTION STEP	WHEN
Jack	Check availability and prices for three conference centers	by next meeting
Cindy	Invite speaker	by February 15
Cheryl	Check calendar to make sure date is open	by next meeting

This approach takes much less time than writing full minutes, and it focuses people's attention on what matters. The important part of the meeting is not so much what was discussed (yes, we'll have a conference) but acting on what was discussed (doing the work necessary to actually hold a conference).

Let me summarize, then, the Miller Method for Meetings: Attach action steps to every project and every item for discussion. Don't move on until you've answered, "Who's responsible for this? Who will do what by when?" In fact, at the end of almost every meeting I lead, I say, "Okay, here are the action steps we've listed." Then I read each step out loud to make sure it's accurate and someone is committed to doing it.

A friend kids me that when I'm in a meeting at work, before long, "The jaws snap shut." Go ahead: call me Jaws. But the only way I can handle so many words at meetings—the only way I can convert discussion into results—is to make sure a decision is made and action is taken. I've tasted results-oriented meetings, and I'll never go back to the other kind.

I should mention, though, that if an issue is controversial or packed with emotion, I won't call for a decision in one meeting. Instead, I'll say, "We're not going to make a final decision today. We're just going to talk it through, raise as many questions as we can, and see what we still need to learn. Then at our next meeting or the one after that, we'll make a final decision." That calms people and keeps them from feeling rushed to judgment. Yes, I'm highly committed to taking action, but I won't do that until the group is ready. It's okay on difficult decisions for your action step to be "Decide at our next meeting."

BOOKS

Here's a scenario that is painfully familiar: Someone hands you a 300-page book and says, "You really ought to read this." Given your relationship, you'd like to please the person who gave you the book, but you don't have time to read it.

"You have a book you'd like me to read, Mrs. Brown?
Why, how thoughtful of you!"

(Source: © 1983 *Leadership*. http://www.LeadershipJournal.net. Concept: David McCasland.
Art: Frank Baginski. Used with permission.)

Your shelf is sagging with books you really ought to read.
What to do?

◇ Decide if the book is in one of your key learning areas or
playful reading you genuinely want to do. If not, thank the
person but don't feel guilty about not reading the book. Only
you, not well-meaning friends, can direct your continuing
education. They may rightly deserve a voice, but you must
cast the final vote.

This is going to lower whatever esteem I once held in your
eyes, but my mother, whom I dearly love, gave me a book four

years ago, and I still haven't read it. She had read and enjoyed it, so she spent considerable money to buy me a copy. When she handed me the book and I read the cover, I agreed it was an important book, a magisterial volume, an interesting read.

But I still haven't read the book.

Mom asks me occasionally, "Did you ever read that book I gave you?"

I pause and somewhat awkwardly confess, "No, sorry, I haven't."

The reason is simple. I've done what novelist Jonathan Franzen has done: "multiplying the number of books I'd read in the previous year by the number of years I might reasonably be expected to live." In both his case and mine, the outcome was a "three-digit product."[4] The painful fact is, even if God allows me to live as long as the actuaries predict, I have time to read only a pathetically tiny number of books. Every book must count. So I keep a list I call "Books That Fit My Learning Areas and That I Want to Read." Rarely will I depart from this list, even though the encouragement to do so comes from my sainted mother. (However, filial devotion might cause me to do what I suggest next.)

() If the recommended book does fall in your key learning areas, but you lack the time to read it, then here's what I do. It's better to read a thirty-page chapter and take one action as a result than to not read the book or to read all three hundred pages and do nothing. So I select the seminal chapter of the book—usually chapter 2 or 3—and based on the ideas presented in that chapter, I take one of the following actions:

- photocopy a few pages for a key leader or staff member who needs the information

- file an illustration or quotation for use in a future class, article, or speech
- write a key thought in my journal or on a Post-it note for my bulletin board, to focus on during the next month
- call a person to discuss the chapter I read or to get more information about the topic
- add an idea to the agenda of an upcoming meeting.

No, I didn't read 270 of the 300 pages, but I did act on something I read and became more effective as a result. That, to me, is success. Plus, I can say to the person who loaned me the book, "I liked the idea of _____, and now I'm doing _____ as a result," which affirms the giver.

() If—wonder of wonders!—you do have the time and desire to read the entire book, find a way to capture the key ideas. (For more on how to capture ideas, see chapter 3.)

When I read Lyle Schaller's *Discontinuity and Hope*, for example, I underlined points that struck me with force. When I finished the book, I reread the underlined sections, then I typed those selections into a file. That final skim reading and typing took about thirty minutes. But my notes later saved me ninety minutes, when I was asked to co-teach a seminar. I wanted to include insights from *Discontinuity and Hope*. Instead of having to flip through the book again, trying to jump-start my memory, I simply opened the file. The best insights had been captured and could immediately be put to use.

REPORTS

You may be one of the fortunates, the blessed, those people who don't receive reports as part of their work. I am not so favored. Every week reports fly into my office and land on my desk: revenue-projection reports, inventory reports, budget-deviation reports, market-research reports, industry reports, reports from people in other departments, and reports from people in my own department. I've often thought, *I can either read those reports or do my job, but I don't have time to do both.*

The overload caused me to skim most reports and put them on the shelf. Nothing really happened as a result. Thousands of dollars went into the making of these reports, yet they produced so little change. It was as if employees had sworn a secret pact: "We will create reports, skim reports, and file reports, but we will never, ever, change as a result of them."

I decided to start asking myself as I read the reports, "So what? What specific action am I going to take as a result of this report?" That two-word question, "So what?" has performed a miracle: I have actually seen the water of reports change into the wine of results.

() *For each report, try to take an action step.* Six times a year our company surveys customers who subscribe to a monthly audio series. That means that six times a year I get a report summarizing how high or low they rated the series. I've seen dozens of these reports over the years, so it's tempting to skim them and then file them. I decided to start taking action steps based on these reports. For example:

1. Because customers had rated the series high on "helpfulness of content," I tore off that page of the report and wrote, "Way to go, team! You're keeping the content helpful to people," and circulated that to the people who created those tapes. The result: they were encouraged.

2. A particular audio segment was highly rated, and I thought, *This could be reprinted and given as a booklet to*

people who choose to renew their subscription. I emailed that idea to our marketing director, who liked it and implemented it.

3. One subscriber asked if he could submit his own tape for possible inclusion in the series. I forwarded his question to an editor who could reply to this question.

4. The report asked about customers' interest in a new product idea. People said they would purchase the new product if we made it available. So I looked at my calendar and set a meeting with the person who would create that new product.

5. Setting that meeting reminded me that I used to meet with this editor monthly but had gotten out of the habit, so I set up monthly meeting dates with him.

Five positive actions from one report. I didn't file anything: the report was in shreds by the time I finished. And I didn't try to remember anything. I simply selected the few most important ideas and acted on those.

() *Break large reports into manageable chunks.* Sometimes we don't take action on reports because they're too large. For example, I ordered from ContentBiz the proceedings of their annual conference. I paid $199 for the report, which struck me as an awful lot of money. I finally justified it by saying, "I'd have paid more than that to attend the conference in person, and my notes wouldn't have been this complete. Plus, if I implement one or two good ideas on boosting subscription sales, that will recoup my investment." You could hear the wheels of justification grinding in my head.

When the report came, though, it was 240 pages thick. I groaned. *I don't have the time to sit and read this.* Then I remembered, *What's important is not so much reading this report but extracting the information we really need and then acting on it.*

I came up with a plan.

The report was about marketing, and there are four people on our marketing team. Add me, and you've got five people. So I asked the marketing director to quickly skim the report's eleven chapters and pick the five that most applied to what we do. Then she would assign one chapter to each of us. We would read the chapter and highlight any great ideas we could apply. Nobody had to write a report or even a summary, just use a highlighter as we read. Then we would meet and discuss these ideas and decide which ones we were going to apply.

This plan, while not necessarily perfect, did what I wanted. It kept the $199 report from sitting on the shelf, collecting dust mites, because no one on our staff had enough time to sit and read 240 pages. It lowered the reading load for any one person to just a single chapter, only about 20 pages. It saved us from having to write or give a report; all we had to do was select—just by marking the text with a highlighter—any ideas we could apply. And finally, the plan got all our key people thinking how we could apply the latest and best strategies.

() *Keep reports simple.* In my experience, most reports give too much information. I used to get budget-deviation reports that were twelve pages of paper, packed with detail. And they included variances that were minuscule: $127. I had to wonder, *Why are we taking the time to report this?*

So I asked the people who prepared these reports to take the following steps to simplify the reports and make them easier to read:

1. Fit everything on one Excel spreadsheet. That's much easier for me to handle than twelve pieces of paper.

2. Rank the spreadsheet from the biggest deviation to the lowest deviation. That way, I can quickly zoom in on the biggest.

3. Show all negative deviations in red, to make them stand out.

4. Include only deviations of significance (in our scale, $1,000 or more).

5. Be honest about the reasons for the budget deviation; if we overestimated sales, then type, "we overestimated sales" in the spreadsheet. No excuses, no blaming.

The people who prepared the reports were happy to make these changes, because the changes saved them work. And the changes saved me time. Budget-deviation reports are now some of the most helpful reports I get, and I actually look forward to reading them. The reports are so simple that it's easy for me to read them and take action—usually, to ask questions about something veering from our budget.

I've probably given too much detail in these examples; after all, your situation may be quite different. But I wanted to show specifically how to take dense reports and convert them into results. If you want to turn information into results, you have to start by asking that magic two-word question, So what? How can I apply what I'm learning? How can a decision be made, an action taken, a matter closed?

In football, the goal is not to march ninety-five yards and turn over the ball on downs; it's to score. By asking, "So what?" you can get into the end zone of applied knowledge.

If all this sounds like too much work, I haven't explained it well. Actually, these simple practices can convert mind-numbing information into heart-stirring accomplishment. You could even call these practices liberating. That's what Craig from Ontario told me after reading these ideas and applying them: "Thank you for your ideas. I found them very liberating. . . . The idea of applying at least one thing from what I read, learn or experience has gone from a frustrating exercise to an attainable goal."[5]

QUESTIONS TO APPLY

- In which area do I feel most overloaded by information: seminars, meetings, books, or reports?

- What is one thing I could do in that area to turn information into results?

QUOTES TO TAKE WITH YOU

" Data, data everywhere, but not a thought to think.

—*Sonya Yespuh*[6]

" Information is not knowledge. You can mass-produce raw data and incredible quantities of facts and figures. You cannot mass-produce knowledge, which is created by individual minds, drawing on individual experience, separating the significant from the irrelevant, making value judgments.

—*Theodore Roszak*[7]

part 2

CLEARING
Information Clutter
Less is more

chapter 5

YOUR INFORMATION AUDIT
How to find out if what you're getting is what you need

Read this chapter if:

❑ You have never examined the information flowing into your life.

❑ You can't keep up with what you need to know or to read for work.

❑ You feel overwhelmed by the news.

Helen Lee started an Internet company in the late '90s, at the height of the web business craze. She recalls: "In this new information economy, knowledge was power, and so you tried to get as much of it as you could to provide you with that competitive edge. In the words of Andy Grove (founder of Intel): *Only the Paranoid Survive.* You had to know if anyone else was starting an idea like yours, who was funding what, what the pitfalls could be, who the key players in the industry were, what technologies were hot. This meant subscribing to and regularly reading the following publications: *Fortune, Forbes, Business Week, The Wall Street Journal, Financial Times, Red Herring, Business 2.0, Inc., Fast Company, Entrepreneur, Wired,* whatever your local paper was, plus the *New York Times.* Every night after I came home from work, I'd feel an obligation to power through as many of these periodicals as I could, but I never could keep up with it all. Trying to do so was impossible, not to mention exhausting."[1]

Though we feel we get too much information and can't keep up, we can't say for sure how much information we really need. We don't know how much information will make us effective. Workers on an assembly line are assigned a defined task—say, pop a rivet into this steel panel—and that task can be measured and timed. Workers in an office today have no easy way to ensure they're being effective. Are they finding the right information and applying it? Is reading that email newsletter productive or a waste of time?

A business executive once lamented to a friend of mine, "I have a doctor to keep me healthy, a CPA to keep me solvent, and an attorney to keep me legal. But who will keep me productive?"

Using this executive's reasoning, we need a doctor's checkup or a CPA's audit on our information life. We must monitor what information we're getting and determine— rigorously—whether we need it. In this chapter, I will show how you can conduct an information audit. You'll probably discover, as I have, that an information audit leads to greater freedom and focus in your life and work.

WHERE TO START YOUR INFORMATION AUDIT

An information audit simply traces the information you're already reading, skimming, listening to, and watching. It finds out what information you're getting and what you're doing with it.

An information audit may sound difficult, but you can do one in less than thirty minutes. And if you're more intuitive and unstructured in your approach, you may do it faster than that. Simply pick a key topic you get information about or need to know. It might be in your profession or it might be an intense hobby, like gardening or golf. (If you've read chapter 2, you've probably already listed key topics for your life.) Pick one topic, and then ask yourself six questions:

1. **Source:** Where am I getting my information?
2. **Frequency:** How often do I receive this information?
3. **Time:** How much time am I spending to get this information?
4. **Value:** How does this information help me?
5. **Need:** Given my information needs, do I still need this information source, or could I live without it?
6. **New approach:** For the information I must have, is there another, quicker way to get it? Is there another person who could gather this information?

I find it easiest to put these questions into a chart. At the end of this chapter, I provide a blank chart for you to photocopy and use (p. 79).

SAMPLE INFORMATION AUDIT: A WORK-RELATED TOPIC

Let me show you two information audits I conducted, so you'll get a feel for how to do them. The first audit was on a topic central to my work: e-commerce. Every day my team helps create paid content for websites. My performance would suffer if I didn't stay up on e-commerce trends and strategies.

Here's what I found when I conducted an information audit on the topic of e-commerce. I listed eight sources in my audit, but to save you time, I have included only four samples.

KEY AREA: E-COMMERCE					
Source	Frequency	Time Spent	Value Grade	Still Need?	New Approach
1. *Email Sherpa* email newsletter	Weekly.	Skim contents. Read 1 article. 10 minutes a week.	C. Love the insight and personality of newsletter, but it's more about email marketing than paid-access websites.	No.	Others on my staff are email marketing specialists: (1) Forward an issue of *Email Sherpa* to them and suggest they subscribe, and (2) invite them to send me articles they find helpful for our work.
2. Major study by Online Publishers Association or similar group	2 times per year.	Read highlights, skim some chapters, read other chapters. 2 hours every 6 months.	A. I need authoritative studies and findings, rather than ephemeral hypotheses. The last OPA report improved our strategy.	Yes.	(1) Schedule a block of time in the next month to read the most recent report. (2) Keep reading offers for these kinds of studies.
3. *Fast Company* magazine	12 times per year.	Read cover, skim table of contents,	Hard to admit this, but D. The magazine is a fun read, but articles	No. (Sigh)	Take my name off the routing slip.

		and read 1–2 articles. 20 minutes a month.	focus on large for-profits like Wal-Mart, and we're a small not-for-profit. Plus, articles focus on corporate culture, not on e-commerce.		
4. NYTimes.com technology section	Visit website 4–5 times per week.	Scan 3 technology headlines each day. Read a total of 3 stories per week. 20 minutes per week.	B-. The stories cover more than e-commerce, but because I can quickly scan the headlines and the reporting is high quality, I do benefit.	Yes.	Keep for now, but an information audit one year from now might change this.

Most important sources: 2 and 4.
Total estimated time I can save: From all eight sources, including some not shown above, approximately three hours every month. Some of that time will be reinvested in the more profitable reading of major studies.

If you're like my friend Rob, who describes himself as "more intuitive," you probably (to quote him) "hate sitting down and spending time conducting any kind of audit on paper." Rob asks, "Is this a bad thing? Am I doomed?"

No, you're not doomed. In fact, you can conduct your audit more quickly. Pick up something in your office—a journal, a magazine, or a printout of an email newsletter—and throw it into one of three piles: Must Read, Probably Should Read, or Not Essential. Pick up another magazine and toss it

onto the appropriate pile. Continue until you're done tossing, and then do two things:

1. Unsubscribe to anything in the Not Essential pile.
   Then throw it away.
2. Look at the Probably Should Read pile. Chances are,
   if you don't read this pile, you won't be censured by
   the U.S. Senate. But emotionally, you're not ready to
   admit that. Fine. You can keep this pile and read it
   whenever you finish the Must Read pile. (Okay, I
   tricked you: that golden moment of reading everything
   in the Must Read pile never comes. Now are you ready
   to throw away your Probably Should Read pile, too?)

Whether you approach your audit formally or informally,
notice several things:

 ℘ *It's easy to think, I don't need to conduct an information
audit.* But when I did the audit on e-commerce, I was surprised to realize just how many sources of information I had.
I would have guessed three or four, and I wound up with
eight. That's because some activities don't immediately seem
like they're "information gathering." You're just looking at the
magazines that come across your desk or reading email, so
you don't count that time, but such time is the heart of most
people's workday.

 ℘ *When asking how valuable an information source is, be ruthlessly honest. What am I doing with this information? Is it really
helping me? How?* If you can't quickly and clearly answer
those questions, the information may not be that valuable.
Assign a grade, from A to F, that describes the value of this
source to *you*. (Or toss it onto the proper pile.)

Then ask yourself, "Is there any way to change what I'm
doing?" For example, by dropping one daily email newsletter

and instead visiting that company's website once per month, I save hours every year.

Also ask, "Could any of the information I need be gathered by someone else?" Notice that for source 1 in the table, the *Email Sherpa* weekly newsletter, I asked three people, who need to focus on its specialized content more than I do, to send me articles from the newsletter that they think I must read. Just yesterday, that happened. Cory, a guy on my team, forwarded an issue of the newsletter containing a great article on cleaning email lists. I read the article and learned a lot; it directly applies to our work and will help us.

As I read that article, I didn't think, *Wow, I didn't see this article, and I could have missed something important.* Instead I felt, *Great! Without my having to read* Email Sherpa, *I still stayed in touch with the article that most applied to our work.*

❡ *An information audit can show you where you're overloading on information.* For example, I had no idea I was receiving twenty-eight email newsletters per month on the subject of e-commerce. Wow. By unsubscribing to some of them, I managed to cut my monthly email newsletters from twenty-eight to four. And so far, I'm still getting sufficient new information on the subject of e-commerce.

William Van Winkle reminds us, "Data is like food. A good meal is served in reasonably-sized portions from several food groups. It leaves you satisfied but not stuffed. Likewise with information, we're best served when we can partake of reasonable, useful portions, exercising discretion in what data we digest and how often we seek it out. Unfortunately, we often do the opposite, ingesting information constantly to the point of choking on it."[2]

❡ *By implementing even a few changes, you can save amazing amounts of time.* From what I learned through my e-commerce information audit, I was able to save thirty-six hours per year—four full workdays! But the precise amount of time doesn't matter as much as the sense of freedom I gain.

SAMPLE INFORMATION AUDIT: THE NEWS

If you can conduct only one information audit, I suggest you choose *news* as your topic. Everyone deals with news, and most of us get too much of it. Writer Scott Rosenberg admits, "By the side of my bed sits a two-foot-high stack of unread newspapers. Its contents may shift, as some papers get read and removed and others get added, but it never vanishes, hard as I try to make headway against the newsprint tide. The stack first appeared when I was in college and has accompanied me ever since; it will probably not disappear until I do."[3]

On pages 75–76, I show my information audit on news. Yours may be radically different, and you may disagree with my reasoning. That's fine. The point is to stop and look at your sources of news.

As you do an information audit on news, pay attention to the following:

❢ *Which type of news is most valuable to you.* For example, Leith Anderson, a pastor, values local news because of his work: "I regularly read the Minneapolis paper, and when I'm traveling, I read *USA Today* or *The Wall Street Journal*. But as a local pastor, it's more important for me to understand the local perspective than to know what's going on someplace else from another perspective."[4]

On the other hand, a professor I know feels precisely the opposite: "I couldn't care less what happens in my town, because I don't own a home there and I don't have kids. I am

KEY AREA: NEWS

Source	Frequency	Time Spent	Value Grade	Still Need?	New Approach
1. NYTimes.com	4–6 times per week.	Read most headlines on home page, read 2–3 stories. 15 minutes a day. About 90 minutes a week.	A. Sure, the *Times* offers more than I need on Manhattan and Tel Aviv, but on topics I need, its reporting is strong.	Yes.	Stay the course, since for me this is faster and more enjoyable than watching news on TV. But limit myself to 1 visit per day, even in times of war or crisis.
2. *Chicago Tribune*	7 days per week.	Read headlines on front page of news, business, regional, and sports sections. Read or skim 3–5 stories. 20 minutes a day plus 45 minutes on Sunday.	C. The local/regional news is nice, but the rest repeats what I read at NYTimes.com.	No.	Drop the daily subscription. For now, keep the Sunday, but reevaluate that in 3 months.
3. *Time* magazine	1 day per week.	Read cover and table of contents, read 3–5 articles. 40 minutes per week.	B-. Gives me a sense of trends in culture, which is helpful.	Yes.	Keep reading, but avoid the basic news stories, which I already read at NYTimes.com

(continued from page 75)					
4. News radio WBBM	5 days per week.	Listen to news while driving to or from work. 50 minutes a week.	D. Same headlines at NYTimes.com, but there, I can read more if I want to.	No.	Better for me to listen to music or, gasp, drive in silence.
5. *Christianity Today*'s email newsletter, *CT Direct*	5 days per week.	Scan headlines, read the weblog. 50 minutes a week.	A. Given my work, it helps to know breaking religion news, and I trust the reporting.	Yes.	Keep for now, but if they offer a weekly version, consider subscribing to that instead.
6. Local newspaper, the *Wheaton Sun*	1 day per week.	Read cover to cover. 30 minutes a week.	A-. Essential for news on the city, the school board, and the park district. But do I need the movie reviews here?	Yes.	Skip the movie reviews, car column, and other nonlocal items. For movies, go to ScreenIt.com instead.

Most important sources: 1, 5, and 6.
Total estimated time I can save: Approximately three hours every week.

much more interested in popular culture, because this helps me relate to my students and my work."

❡ *The total amount of time you're spending on news.* When I finished my news audit, I had to ask myself if I could honestly say, "My life is so much richer because I'm spending over seven hours on news every week." Seven hours is overkill.

Nathan Shedroff explains, "We have built our culture and institutions around the rapid, even instantaneous, delivery of data labeled as important and worthy of vast amounts of our time, yet it serves almost no importance in our lives."[5]

In my case, by dropping my daily subscription to the *Chicago Tribune* (it mostly repeats the news I get online), and by turning off the all-news radio station (which doesn't give in-depth news coverage), I save nearly three hours every week, and I still know the major news events in the world. Think about this: by making two small adjustments I will gain 156 hours in the coming year. That is almost a solid week I can add back into my life. Think what I could do with that time. I could talk with my son or daughter or wife. I could pray. I could take a catnap, go on a walk, play basketball in my driveway. These wonderful activities too often get squeezed out, and now the discipline of an information audit is beginning to restore them to me.

What proportion of your news comes through TV. Though it's the primary news source for Americans, TV news has limitations:

1. With the Internet or a newspaper, you can select the news stories that help you the most. Unfortunately, with TV, you have no power over which news stories get covered. If the producer thinks, say, that a three-alarm fire deserves major coverage, you're stuck with that. If you love watching news, better to use RealOne Player (http://www.real.com) and select the news videos you need most from the FeedRoom.

2. TV news gives an inaccurately high perception of violence in our world. "Seventy-seven percent of the lead stories on television news programs are reporting events

of crime or violence."[6] That's because, as Barry Glassner explains, "Television news programs survive on scare. On local newscasts, where producers live by the dictum, 'If it bleeds, it leads,' drug, crime and disaster stories make up most of the news portion of the broadcasts. . . . Between 1990 and 1998, when the nation's murder rate declined by 20%, the number of murder stories on network newscasts increased by 600%."[7]

3. Weather and commercials now make up nearly half of each hour's broadcast.[8]

If you audit the news sources in your life, and I hope you will, your answers will be different from mine. You will find solutions that work for you. To aid you in that process, I've included a blank chart that you can photocopy or adapt to your needs (p. 79).

You may not be an analytical person, and charts like this make your eyes glaze over. That's fine; you don't have to use a chart. The key to an information audit is not a certain chart; the key is occasionally looking at the information flowing into your life. Maybe you think best when you're talking, and so the best way for you to conduct an information audit is to talk with a friend. But whatever approach you take, have the courage to ask, *Do I need all this information?*

If the answer is no—and the answer is almost always no—then take out your pruning shears. You'll be glad you did.

One self-confessed "news junkie" told me, "I'm learning that I can control the information flow that comes my way. It doesn't have to control me. And it's really rare that I need the flow to be as large as it can be, which is infinitely large. Now I have a much more narrow flow, yet I don't feel I'm missing out on anything."

MY INFORMATION AUDIT
KEY AREA:

Source	Frequency	Time Spent	Value Grade	Still Need?	New Approach

Most important sources:

Total estimated time I can save:

QUESTIONS TO APPLY

- What would be the ideal way for me to conduct an information audit: using the chart in this chapter, talking with someone, or another approach?

- What topic—news, a work-related topic, or something else—should I audit first?

- Can I stop and do an audit right now? If not, can I block half an hour in the next two weeks when I can?

QUOTES TO TAKE WITH YOU

" I'm more and more tired of paper, and more and more interested in the people I live with and among.

—*Barbara Brown Taylor*[9]

" Transformation is less about what you decide to do and more about what you decide not to do.

—*Eirik Olsen*[10]

chapter 6

HOW TO HANDLE EMAIL

Changing your inbox from curse to blessing

Read this chapter if:

❑ You spend more than thirty minutes per day reading or writing email.

❑ You're frustrated with spam or other unwanted email.

❑ You find that email is distracting you from more important work.

I can picture myself at a support group, admitting, "Hi, I'm Kevin. I'm an email addict."

"Welcome, Kevin," the group says.

"I don't know where to begin," I say, looking down. "My troubles started without my knowing it. We were all on slow dial-up then—14.4. Many people still sent information the old-fashioned way, in a paper envelope. That's hard to remember now."

"Go on," they say.

"I didn't mean to get hooked. It's just that it was so easy to send email—to forward it, to reply immediately, wowing the person who had just sent it. I had no idea it would take over my life."

One man in the corner nods his head knowingly. "I understand," he says.

"It all seemed so innocent. The jokes, the FYIs, the requests for a meeting time, and now—now . . ." my voice trails off to a whisper. "Now I read email all day long. It keeps me from doing the work I should be doing. My day is run by the inbox in Microsoft Office. I am powerless to help myself."

I haven't actually attended an EE meeting—Emailers E-nonymous—but I confess my addiction to email. I know it's irrational, but I simply must clear out my inbox. How sweet to answer emails immediately. I feel productive, clean, responsive, in control. Never mind that this is not efficient, that I should never let my day and priorities be determined by the order that emails happen to be received. I can't seem to accept that many of my emails are the equivalent of spam: many don't need to be answered right away, and others don't need to be answered ever.

I have tried to change my dark attraction to reading and replying to email, and I've found it's harder than I thought it would be. I finally realized, *If a toddler is tempted by a cookie jar, reason won't do. You need to lift the cookie jar up and out of reach. I need strategies that keep my eyes out of the inbox.*

If you don't have strategies for handling your email, you soon will. According to the Pew Internet and American Life Survey, your volume of email is going up (48 percent of respondents say their volume of work email has increased over the past year) or staying the same (46 percent), but it's probably not going down (only 6 percent).[1]

My goal is to move from "possessed emailer" to "productive emailer." Let me define these terms so you'll know where you are now and where you can be (see table).[2]

A while back I conducted a fearless and searching inventory of my email habits, and the numbers sobered me. On average, I received fifty-three emails every workday. I wrote and sent thirty-one. I left my email program always open and checked it four or more times per hour, sometimes constantly. No wonder the heart of my workday—three and a half hours!—was cut out by email.

This is beyond possessed; this is *Exorcist* level.

I had to ask myself, "How productive can I be when I'm spending the best hours of my day answering email—when I could be planning, casting vision, meeting with key people?" I also had to ask a question of moral responsibility: "Since I'm being paid to lead, am I returning to my employer a good return on that investment? Or am I frittering away my time and energies on secondary activities?"

	Possessed Emailer (20 percent of all work emailers)	Productive Emailer (70 percent of all work emailers)
Number of messages received per workday	35–50 or more	5–20
Number of messages sent per workday	12–30 or more	3–12
Number of times per workday email is checked	3–4 times per hour; email program always open	1–2 times per day
Hours per workday spent on email	2–4 hours or more	Less than 1 hour

These rhetorical questions hung in my brain. They forced me to develop—with difficulty but with growing success—nineteen power strategies that help me control the email and keep the email from controlling me.

Since implementing some of these strategies, I've cut my inbound emails by 27 percent. I've lowered my outbound emails by 15 percent. I've gained more than forty-five minutes in every workday. I'm well on my way from being a possessed emailer to being a productive emailer, and I'm continuing to make improvements. Wherever you are in that process, you can use these power strategies to become more effective and to save time.

I wish someone had shared these strategies with me earlier. But since this is a longer chapter, I recommend you skim the nineteen ideas and read only the ones that will work for you. Even one or two ideas, regularly implemented, can make a big difference.

Power Strategy 1: When you need to concentrate on something important, close your email program.

Too many times just as I start working on a major project, I get the sudden urge to see if there are emails in my inbox. This animal urge must be obeyed, or so it seems. By the time I answer those emails, though, I forget where I am on the major project, and I have to start over. What a waste of time and precious mental energy.

Now when I want to focus on a project, I close my email program.

According to the Pew Internet and American Life Survey, about a third of all work emailers say email has made them too accessible to others.[3] There's a solution. Go ahead, move your mouse to the upper right corner and click on the X. As Bob the Builder would say, "You can DO it!"

✉ Power Strategy 2: Answer email during your off times, not your peak times.

Most workers—82 percent—try to answer email "they *should* respond to" by the end of the day.[4] I likewise want to answer most of my email the day I receive it. But nothing dictates *when* during the day I must reply. When I answer should be determined not by when I receive the email but by the rhythm and needs of my day.

For example, I have the most energy from 7:30 to 10:30 in the morning. Then I slump slightly, feeling less energy until about 2:30 in the afternoon, when I get a second wind. It makes sense to schedule my biggest projects—writing an article, planning for a meeting—for my high-energy hours in the morning or late afternoon. I can easily read and answer email with the lower concentration I feel in the off hours.

Your peak and off-peak hours will be different, of course. But identify your lower-energy times and relegate your email work to those hours. H. Dale Burke says, "I've found it helpful to answer all my email at the end of the day. I was surprised how much faster I process it when my family is waiting for me. The bell that signals 'You've got mail' isn't nearly as important as my arrival home that signals to my family, 'You've got Dad.'"[5]

(If you, like me, need to answer email more than once a day, pick an off time during the morning and another during the afternoon for this task. Or if you truly must answer email frequently during the day, then when you start your day, complete one non-email project before you turn to your email.)

📧 *Power Strategy 3: Turn off the sound for incoming emails.*

The Pew Internet and American Life Survey found that nearly a third of all work emailers find email distracting at times.[6] Says Gwen Miller, a mortgage broker in northern Virginia: "When I'm working on a project or writing something I need to finish, email pops up and totally interrupts the writing I'm doing."

I've found it helpful to reduce the distraction by muting the sound on my incoming email. If I don't hear the sound, I'm not as likely to stop what I'm doing and check the inbox.

> (In Outlook, you can silence your incoming email this way: Tools → Options → Preferences tab → under the Email section, click Email Options . . . → under Message handling, click Advanced Email Options. . . → under When new items arrive, uncheck the box for Play a sound.)

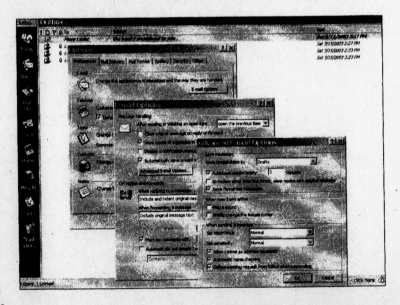

⏴ Power Strategy 4: Space your email deliveries farther apart.

I never gave a thought to how often my email is delivered. Its arrival was a magical, mystical trick—unseen, uncontrolled, and uncontrollable. I never considered that the delivery timing had been set and could be changed.

When I bothered to check, I found my email was being delivered every ten minutes! No wonder that as soon as I finished answering one or two emails, another one arrived, and I got caught in an endless read-and-answer loop. I had to ask, "Are these emails so important that they simply must be delivered every ten minutes?" The answer: no. Some emails required a quick reply, but for none would a delay jeopardize national security.

I spaced my deliveries thirty minutes apart, and that simple switch pushed me to answer my emails in batches, which has proven to be a more efficient use of my time.

(In Outlook 2000, set your delivery time this way: Tools → Options → Mail Delivery tab → under Mail account options, click Check for new messages every ____ minutes and use the up or down arrow to change the number of minutes.)

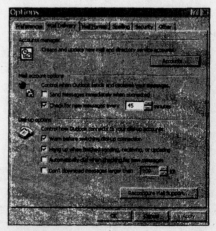

(In Outlook 2002, choose Tools → Send/Receive Settings → Define Send/Receive Groups → click on All Accounts. Then, under Setting for group "All Accounts," check the box for Schedule an automatic send/receive every ___ minutes and use the up or down arrow to change the number of minutes. Conveniently, Outlook 2002 allows you to set different times for different types of accounts.)

Power Strategy 5: Ask people not to "Reply to All" when meetings are being set up.

Email can be a quick and efficient way to set up a meeting. But what often happens is that each of the six people invited hits "Reply to All." So instead of getting one or two emails, you get six more emails, each saying something that doesn't help you: "I can't come on Tuesday."

At your next department or team meeting, gently request that when people are invited to a meeting, they reply only to the meeting organizer. If some of them actually listen to the suggestion, you'll save yourself dozens of emails every month.

Power Strategy 6: Make the most of spam filters.

I sit at my desk and need to get work done. When I open my email, I find: "Apply for an online mortgage loan AA," "Married but lonely people want you," and "Get prescribed Viagra, Diet Pills, and much more online! Overnight Shipping." *Time* reported a Jupiter Research forecast that "you will receive 2,257 pieces of 'commercial e-mail' by the end of the year, 60 percent of them unwanted spam and the rest from merchants you've given permission to contact you. By 2006, both kinds will double."[7] The painful reality: spam may make up 45 percent of your work email and up to 70 percent of your email at home.[8]

That spam is taking my valuable time. Jakob Nielsen calls spam "Attention Theft."[9] To be able to work, I need to be shielded by a spam filter. I can set up three lines of defense.

My first and best defense is to choose an Internet service provider that already filters spam, such as MSN, Earthlink, or AOL, which in one day alone blocked 2.4 billion spam emails.[10]

My second line of defense is to choose an email program, such as Bloomba, that offers robust spam filtering. For example, new Macintosh computers come with an email program that blocks spam well. Here are notes on several other major email programs:

- Yahoo's filter automatically moves suspected junk mail into a Bulk folder. I can review what's in that folder, in case a desired email accidentally got sent there, or I can empty the entire folder with a click.

- Outlook automatically filters for junk mail and adult content. The filters send emails with salacious subject lines directly to the Deleted Items folder. When junk mail does make it through the filter—some always does—I can add that sender to a junk-senders list. Every future email from that address will be trashed. In your inbox, simply right-click on the email subject line, pull down to Junk E-mail, then pull over to Add to junk senders list. (The shortcut for this: right-click, J, J.) I now have 317 senders on my junk-senders list, and I avoid all the emails they send. It feels good to know I will never read another email from hahaha@sexy.net.

- Some spammers figured out how to get around this defense: every time they send you spam, they use a different email address. To stop them, I ask my email program to block emails that contain certain words in the subject line, including *Viagra*, *mortgage*, and crude sexual terms.

(In Outlook 2002: Tools ➔ Rules Wizard ➔ New ➔ select Start from a blank rule ➔ select Check messages when they arrive ➔ Next ➔ check With *specific words* in the subject ➔ In the lower pane, click on *Specific words*, enter the words that you want blocked, then click Add. Do that for as many words as you want, then click OK. Rules Wizard walks you through the rest of the process. You can also save a few steps this way: Tools ➔ Rules Wizard ➔ New ➔ select Start creating a rule from a template ➔ select Move messages based on content.)

My third line of defense, which is now necessary for most people, is to buy and install an additional antispam software program. Which one? *Consumer Reports* recommends the following:

- SAProxy Pro by Stata Labs (bloomba.com; $30; an upgraded version built on one that *Consumer Reports* said "outperformed the others.")
- SpamCatcher (mailshell.com/spamcatcher; $30 + $10 yearly fee).
- Spam Sleuth (bluesquirrel.com; $30 + $10 yearly fee).
- *PC* magazine chose as its top program Norton Anti Spam 2004 (symantec.com/antispam; $40).

I've found protected bliss using the free program PopFile (http://popfile.sourceforge.net/). I like the filter because, as Rich Tatum, an email expert at ChristianityToday.com, told me, "The tool takes a few days to train (maybe 5 or 10 minutes a day), but it's amazingly accurate after you've gotten it trained. My installation is currently 96 percent accurate in identifying spam—it knows that *Kevin* and *Miller* are words mostly likely to appear in my normal email, while *sex* and *growth* tend to appear in spam email."

📧 *Power Strategy 7: Set up a secondary email account for purchasing things online.*

The Internet makes it easy to search for and buy things—airplane tickets, books, even parts for electric razors. I like that. What I don't like is the increase of junk email that follows visits to these sites. Most sites are wholly reputable and don't sell my email address, but they add me to their special emailings, most of which I don't need. Take Ticketmaster. I bought concert tickets from their online site, and now I receive several emails a month with subject lines like "Don't miss Jimmy Buffett." Since I don't attend many concerts in a year, and I could miss Jimmy Buffett without disappointment, that email merely distracts me from my work.

Retailers will always send me follow-up emails, but I can reduce junk mail by having those sent to a secondary account.

By the way, despite a new law prohibiting it, spammers often harvest email addresses from public websites. So if you must list your (secondary) email address on a public site such as eBay, don't use the @ symbol; write *Kevin at Ameritech.net* rather than *Kevin@Ameritech.net*.

The next three power strategies—8, 9, and 10—are the most technically involved, but stay with them, because they can really help streamline your email.

📧 *Power Strategy 8: Automatically gather emails by category.*

An assembly line increases efficiency because it asks a worker to focus on one task, to do it repeatedly, which allows the worker to gain speed and facility. Similarly, efficiency comes to our email work when we gather like emails and handle those in a group.

For example, I set up my email program to automatically send all email newsletters to a folder (creatively called Newsletters). I now get through my daily email much quicker. Then, every week or two, when I'm ready for more leisurely and educational reading, I go to the Newsletters folder.

Likewise, you might gather all emails from a certain person or department. Doris Igna, a retired accountant in Ontario, says, "I sort email. . . . This way I deal with the most important first, and can go back to the others when I have time."[11]

> (Here's how to sort your email. In Outlook or Outlook Express, use the Rules Wizard: Tools → Rules Wizard → click New → select Check messages when they arrive → Next → select Where my name is in

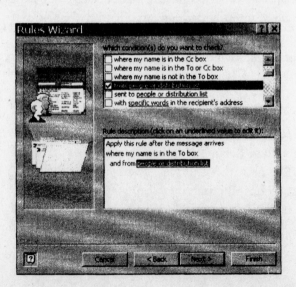

the To box; also select From *people or distribution list*.
In the lower pane, click on *people or distribution list*,
enter the address of the emails you want moved to a
folder, then click OK. Rules Wizard walks you
through the rest of the process. In Outlook 2002, you
can save steps: Tools ➜ Rules Wizard ➜ New ➜ select
Start creating a rule from a template ➜ select Move
new messages from someone.)

You can even set up Outlook to move a *copy* of incoming emails to certain folders. One guy I know likes that
approach because then, he says, "I can safely zap everything
that seems to be of low importance without fear of missing
something important—that stuff gets automatically archived
to my folders."

(Select Tools ➜ Rules Wizard ➜ New ➜ Next ➜
select From *people or distribution list* ➜ in the lower
box, click on *people or distribution list* ➜ select the
people to whom you want to assign a high priority
➜ double-click on the name or click From ➜ OK ➜
Next ➜ select Move a copy to the specified *folder*
➜ in the lower box, click on *folder* and assign where
the copies should go. Rules Wizard will guide you
through the final steps.)

✏ *Power Strategy 9: Highlight emails from important people.*
I recently realized—I don't know why it took me so
long—that email from certain people deserves special attention. So I set up my email program to automatically highlight
email from key people. An email from my wife is turned
bright purple. An email from one of my key managers shows

up bright blue. These colored emails stand out in my inbox, and I read them first.

> (In Outlook: Tools → Organize → Using Colors → under Color messages, select From, type in sender's name, and use the drop-down box to assign a color.)

A more powerful variation of this strategy is to assign high importance to email from certain people and low importance to others. For example, as an Internet operations manager in Illinois explains, "There are maybe five people who regularly communicate with me by email and who can truly set my agenda: my boss, my three employees, and my wife." So using Rules Wizard, he assigns email from those five people a high priority status. Those emails show up in his inbox with a bright red exclamation point, and he works on those first.

On the other hand, he assigns a low priority status to any newsletters or emails from companies. A blue down arrow shows up next to each of these emails.

> (To assign high or low priority to incoming emails: Tools → Rules Wizard → New → Next → select From *people or distribution list* → in the lower box, click on *people or distribution list* → select the people to whom you want to assign a high priority → double-click on the name or click From → OK → Next → select Mark it as *importance* → in the lower box, click on *importance* → in the drop-down box, select High → OK → Next → add any exceptions you desire to this rule → Next → Finish.)

What really makes this system powerful is that you can group all your messages by priority. All the high-priority emails show up together, then all the normal priority, and finally, at the bottom of your inbox, all the low-priority emails.

(To do this in Outlook, simply click on the Importance field in your inbox header—the exclamation point. If you don't see an exclamation point in your inbox header, you can add that feature: View ➜ Current View ➜ Customize Current View ➜ Fields ➜ in the lefthand box, select Importance ➜ Add ➜ OK.)

You can even set up your inbox so that it *always* groups your emails by importance. This approach allows you to "collapse" a category—usually the low-priority emails—so you see only the category's title and don't have to look at the emails inside. In fact, you can delete a category, and all the emails in that category are automatically deleted.

(In Outlook's inbox: View ➜ Current View ➜ Customize Current View ➜ Group by ➜ in the drop-down box, select Importance ➜ OK.)

Power Strategy 10: Automate your email practices.
Now that you know how to use the Rules Wizard, you can automate almost any email function you do more than once.

For example, I receive a weekly email from my daughter's band director. The information is meant for my daughter, Anne, but since she doesn't check her email daily, we had the emails sent to me. I print them and drop them in my briefcase to take home to Anne. Since this happened regularly, I created a process in Rules Wizard that automatically prints any emails from the band director; the subject line of the email then changes to red to let me know it's been printed.

Or suppose you include your phone and address with every email you send. You can create a signature with that information and have it automatically sent in each email.

(To create a signature in Outlook 2000: Tools → Options → Mail Format tab → under Signature section, click Signature Picker → New. To use that signature in every new email: Tools → Options → Mail Format tab → under Signature section, make sure the name of your signature is in the box next to Use this signature by default. In Outlook 2002, the steps are slightly different: Tools → Options → Mail Format tab → under Signature section, click Signatures... → New. To use that signature in every new email: Tools → Options → Mail Format tab → under Signature section, make sure the name of your signature is in the box next to Signature for new messages. You can choose a different signature for replies and forwards.)

Alternately, you could have Outlook attach your business card to each email you send so the recipient can add it to his or her address book.

(Here's how: Tools → Options → Mail Format tab → under Signature section, click Signature Picker (or Signatures...) → New → under Card options, select New vCard from contact → then select your own address.)

I highly recommend using such tools. They're great aids, yet only 10 percent of workers use them, or even know about them.[12]

🖅 *Power Strategy 11: Use a preview feature or scan headers.*

When I read paper mail at home, I have no qualms about throwing away junk mail unopened. Why should I read, say, an appeal from an unknown charity when my wife and I have already agreed to a charitable-giving plan, one that focuses on known charities working on issues we care about? I toss the envelope and save the time required to open it.

Oddly, I don't feel the same freedom with email. Somehow email feels more personal, more intimate. And with email, the "envelope" has already been opened; I can start reading right away.

But I have trained myself to scan subject lines. If I don't know the sender, and the subject line is quirky, I hit Delete. For example, today I received an email from "Christopher Carver," a name I didn't recognize. The subject line read: "Fwd: No prior prescription required." I didn't need to read further; I hit Delete. That saved me the bother of reading "Order prescriptions from the largest U.S. company specializing in VIAGRA" blah blah blah.

Don't read full-screen email after full-screen email. By scanning your inbox or using the preview pane (in Outlook's inbox: View → Preview Pane), you can save considerable time. Once in Preview Pane, simply press your scroll bar to read through an email and then advance to the next email. You can even go backward by using Shift + the scroll bar. Beautiful.

Finally, if you like to read a little more than the subject line—say, the first few lines of the email—Outlook has another feature for you: AutoPreview. Check it out. (View → AutoPreview.)

Power Strategy 12: Send fewer emails so you get fewer emails.

This strategy might sound crazy. I need to send email to do my job, so how could I possibly send less of it?

But think with me. Do I really need to copy Jim on this email? If it's not essential he know the information, wouldn't he appreciate not getting an extra email? And then Jim won't send me an email saying, "Thanks," and then I won't send an email saying, "No problem." My innocent "cc:" created three emails when there could have been zero. Thomas A. Stewart wryly comments that "approximately 610 billion e-mails are sent per year, of which at least a third are cc'd to me."[13]

So now I don't automatically add someone to a cc: line. I don't write an email that says "Thanks" merely to acknowledge I received an email. (If I want to thank someone, I take the time to specify what I appreciated.) I don't reply, "No problem." This simple discipline saves me about ten outbound and five inbound emails every week.

Stanley Bing humorously but wisely reminds us, "Close your eyes and ask yourselves: Is the e-mail I'm about to send necessary? And if not, is it at least fun? If you cannot answer yes to either of those questions—don't hit that send button. Electronic flatulence must cease!"[14]

📧 *Power Strategy 13: Save and reuse replies you send often.*

If you're like me, you often get similar questions, which means you often send similar replies. Save those and reuse them. Recycling is a beautiful thing.

> (There are many ways to save and reuse email replies, but here's one I like. In Outlook, save the reply in the Drafts folder. To reuse it, open a new email and then select Insert ➔ Item ➔ under Insert as, select Text only ➔ in the upper box, select the Drafts folder ➔ in the lower box, select the reply you want ➔ OK.)

If you must draft an original email, keep it short to save time. One heavy emailer I know says, "If you're writing for publication, sure, knock yourself out. But for an email that will be discarded upon receipt or (more likely) ignored for days, it just doesn't pay. So I've shortened my normal writing style dramatically."

📧 *Power Strategy 14: Change your email address.*

Almost one-third of email addresses are changed or discontinued every year.[15] Unless your company protocols require you to keep the same address, change your address periodically. Why? It gives your address a clean slate; you immediately and gloriously become invisible to senders of chain letters, virus hoaxes, and bad jokes, who had your old address.

📧 *Power Strategy 15: If possible, have someone else read your email.*

The great thing about email is that anyone can receive it. The bad thing about email is that anyone can receive it. Handling correspondence, which used to be the province of entry-level office assistants, is now being done by executives earning $135,000 per year. Does that make sense?

If you're blessed enough to have someone else on your staff or team who can handle email, use that option. When I was editor of *Leadership*, I observed that 60 to 70 percent of my emails were simple requests for information, which could be handled with standard replies. There were three basic responses: (1) Potential contributors wanted our journal's writer guidelines; (2) readers wanted to say, "Thanks for such-and-such article," and know their email had been received; and (3) people who had sent an article wanted a reply, which most of the time, regrettably, was "We're sorry that we're not able to publish your article." So I asked a bright and capable editorial assistant to read my email first. With modest amounts of training, she was able to answer two-thirds of my email without my having to see it. The remainder required specialized replies from me, and those she forwarded. I saved hours every week, and people got quicker replies. Glory, hallelujah.

In my current job, my email spans a much wider range of requests, and I couldn't easily have someone else handle it for me. But when I write a column for *Leadership Weekly*, our weekly email newsletter, I ask readers to reply to a central email address, not to my personal one. I still try to answer every reply, but if I get swamped, I have the option of asking someone else to respond to these emails.

Power Strategy 16: Limit your involvement in newsgroups.

Newsgroups offer the promise that you'll discuss important ideas with people who share your passions and interests. The reality is that newsgroups send you five extraneous emails for every valuable one. As William Van Winkle explains, "Newsgroups can consume your life. I used to lurk and contribute in half a dozen groups. Today, I only visit Usenet for research, targeting specific answers and ignoring all other conversation threads."[16]

If you're involved in more than two newsgroups, you're probably receiving more emails than you really need. Stanley Bing advises, "We're like junkies who started off with a little recreational pot in the '80s and are now mainlining a couple ounces of horse every day. Well, it's time to hit the e-hab!"[17]

Power Strategy 17: OHIO.

Seminars on dealing with piles of paper recommend "OHIO: Only Handle It Once." And as Jesse Berst writes, "That's good advice for managing email, too. Once a message arrives, read it and act on it. Delete it. Respond to it. File it."[18]

Carla, the editor of a parenting magazine, swears by this advice: "Answering e-mails the moment I get them is key for me. If I let them go even for a day, I forget about them, and then it could be months before I get back to them."

If you can't handle an email just once, flag it for follow-up. That way, you'll know not to read the email a second time.

(In Outlook 2000: select Actions ➜ Flag for Follow Up. In Outlook 2002: select Actions ➜ Follow Up.)

📧 *Power Strategy 18: Revert to print subscriptions for your favorite publications.*

When the CEO of a *website* says, "Print publishing is back in style," I take note. Charles Henderson, head of NewsRX.com, "thinks the future, for now anyway, is still print. Professionals are back subscribing to print newsletters in huge numbers." Why? Henderson speculates, "I figure recipients are probably getting too much email and far less postal mail than they have in years. So the little postal mail they do get, gets increased attention."[19]

The fact is, print is better for longer reading. One study reported that 50 percent of email newsletters were skimmed or read partly, and another 27 percent were not even opened.[20] For sources of information you value, switch back to print. You'll find print easier to read.

Whenever you need to get a grip on a subject, print usually beats email. Tammy, a human resources manager for a major accounting firm, remembers when she was named project manager. "I was getting e-mail from a million different sources. I had serious deadlines and had to make quick decisions based on all of this information. The quantity of information and the speed at which it was coming at me was completely overwhelming.

"So I printed out the emails I felt were pertinent. I literally crossed out nonessential information and highlighted the practical. From that I started a 'need to know' document. I summarized my hard-copy information into short statements that made sense to me and that I could refer to later."

Power Strategy 19: Use face-to-face meetings or the phone for deeper communication.

Is it really a shock that 22 percent of workers report that email has "caused misunderstandings"?[21] Email can't convey tone of voice, it can't capture facial expressions (sorry, smiley faces and other emoticons like ;^D don't help much), and its intensely brief format often comes across as abrupt or harsh. Email works beautifully for simple conversations like confirming a meeting. But if the issue is sensitive, you need to pick up the phone or meet face-to-face.

One manager told me, "Remember, handling a potentially emotional issue in person may feel like a time-sink because it takes half an hour to talk it out, but it will save untold hours of sweating over the proper email phrasing so that nobody's offended—and save even more hours repairing relationships after everybody misreads the carefully crafted Magna e-Carta."

For sensitive situations, face-to-face saves time. That's counterintuitive but true.

Since I've listed nineteen email strategies that work, let me also mention four common strategies that don't work, at least not yet.

Doesn't-Work-Now Strategy 1: Send your address to an email-preferences clearinghouse.

This clearinghouse will then remove your name from commercial email lists, the theory goes. But in practice it usually fails. Why? Often the address where you're told to send your email is inaccurate (for example, an email sent to the published address remove@cyberpromo.com merely comes back as undeliverable). The best site to use is the Direct Marketing Assocation's Email Preference Service (e-MPS) at http://www.dmaconsumers.org/consumers/optoutform_emps.shtml. Submitting your email address keeps it off the list of reputable mailers who adhere to the DMA's guidelines. Unfortunately, many spammers don't use these lists or abide by the DMA's guidelines. The Federal Trade Commission may create a "do not spam" list, but until then, don't expect relief from spam.

Doesn't-Work-Now Strategy 2: Send an unsubscribe request to the spammer.

According to the Federal Trade Commission, only one-third of requests to be taken off spammers' lists were honored.[22] Why? While reputable companies from whom you've bought something have an incentive to not annoy you, other spammers could care less. Think about the type of person who spends his day writing and sending millions of emails on how to enhance your sexual organs. Is this person likely to honor your sincere unsubscribe request? If anything, your response shows you are a responsive emailer and, therefore, one to keep. So save yourself the time of sending an unsubscribe request and simply add the sender to your junk-senders list.

Doesn't-Work-Now Strategy 3: Hope that companies develop sophisticated, new email-processing software.

Will software save us from ourselves?

New software may increase our ability to handle email. Banter, a San Francisco–based firm, is testing software that learns how to sort email based on your behavior. For example, if you immediately read any message from your boss that has the word *deadline* in the text, the software will start placing emails from your boss at the top of your inbox and will even mark them in a different color. If you usually ignore emails from Human Resources, the program will start delivering those to the bottom of your inbox.[23]

To halt spam, a start-up company, Mailblocks, is creating a "challenge-response mechanism." According to John Markoff in the *New York Times*, Mailblocks works like this: "When a customer receives a new message from an unknown correspondent, the system will intercept the message and automatically return to the sender a digital image of a seven-digit number and a form to fill out. Once a human being views that number and types it into the form—demonstrating that he or she is a person and not an automated mass-mailing machine—the system will forward the e-mail to the intended recipient."[24]

Until then, most antispam software uses Bayesian filters that score emails before you see them, adding or subtracting points based on criteria. If the email uses the name of a sexual organ, that adds 75 points. If, on the other hand, the email comes from someone whose address is in your address book, that subtracts 90 points, making it extremely rare that an intended email would accidentally get deleted.

For the foreseeable future, though, the spammers will keep winning. *Newsweek* concludes, "Antispam tools are outmatched."

Doesn't-Work-Now Strategy 4: Wait for Congress or the courts to stop spam.

The United States Congress recently passed antispam legislation, the Can-Spam Act of 2003. Not that it matters much. According to *Consumer Reports*, even tough laws "may not be effective. That's because taking legal action against perpetrators can be extremely difficult."[25] Take, for example,

Delaware: it passed an antispam law in 1999 but hasn't prosecuted anyone since then, largely because the offending emails are sent from international locations.[26]

Experts at a recent Spam Conference held at MIT agreed that the Can-Spam Act "has done nothing to reduce the amount of spam on the Internet."[27] So no matter how sophisticated the laws and the software become, we still need to ask the challenging question: "Is the way I'm using email really helping me be more productive?" If the answer is "I'm not sure it is," then the solution will be implementing strategies like the nineteen above. Here's encouragement from a friend of mine: "I spend less time sending email now than I used to, having adopted some of the strategies you recommended."[28]

QUESTIONS TO APPLY

- Which two power strategies in this chapter would help me most?

- When can I start to implement these?

QUOTES TO TAKE WITH YOU

" Spam costs an estimated $1 per piece in lost productivity.
—*Pew Internet and American Life Project Survey*[29]

" When you have accomplished your daily task, go to sleep in peace; God is awake.
—*Victor Hugo*

HOW TO FIND
WHAT YOU NEED ONLINE

Five principles to guide you through the Internet thicket

Read this chapter if:

❑ You search the web two or more times per week.

❑ You get many results that aren't what you're looking for.

"The Internet is exploding with empty dazzle," explains Richard Saul Wurman, "sites that direct you to nonexistent links, send you down fruitless paths, and generally don't help you get where you want to go.... Several studies have found that somewhere between 60 and 80 percent of people searching for information on the Web failed to find what they were looking for."[1]

And we thought the Internet was supposed to be the mother of all information, the answer to all our information needs. Instead, it frustrates us most of the time—60 to 80 percent of the time. How ironic.

Still, by knowing how to properly search the web, we can flip that statistic upside down: we can *find* what we're looking for 60 to 80 percent of the time. Here are five tips for more successful web searches. By using these principles, you're highly likely to find what you're looking for online—in the first page of results.

🖰 *1. Choose the right search engine for the job.*

Google.com is still the best all-purpose search engine. But the Internet offers many other search engines, some of which outperform Google on certain tasks. Let me recommend which search engine to use when.

When you want the **widest possible search:**

- **HotBot.com** lets you select from four search engines: HotBot, Google, Lycos, and AskJeeves. (HotBot also lets you filter out offensive content, change the look of results pages, and save your search preferences.)
- **Gigablast.com** is simple to use, and if you don't find what you want, each results page allows you to search in six other search engines, including Google and Wisenut.

Faster than those are the metasearch engines, which search many search engines in one pass:

- **Dogpile.com** fetches results from six search engines, including Google and Yahoo. (Too bad its sponsored links look just like the noncommercial ones.)
- **Metacrawler.com** covers eight search engines: Google, Yahoo, AskJeeves, About, Looksmart, FindWhat, Overture, and Altavista. (The Exact Phrase feature doesn't appear to work, however.)

Even better, choose your own list of search engines, directories, and news sites to search—in one pass:

- **Mamma.com** (www.mamma.com/psearch.html) is good, and **Vivisimo.com** (http://vivisimo.com/form? form=Advanced) is better, because it lets you search sites like eBay, CNN, and Britannica. (If you want the ultimate in search coverage and don't mind software adventures, download the free Internet browser **Mozilla Firefox** (www.mozilla.org/products/firefox). Firefox lets you download free plug-ins to search more than one hundred search engines, reference sites, and more (www.texturizer.net/firefox/extensions).

For **news:**

- **News.Google.com** searches 4,500 news sources—and adds breaking news to its home page continuously.
- For European and international news, **uk.newsbot.msn.com** works similarly.

For **books and magazines:**

- **Amazon.com** allows you to search the text of more than 120,000 books. Click the Books tab and then use the Search Books tool at the top of the left column.
- **LookSmart.com** offers 3.5 million magazine articles from more than 700 publications. Just click the Articles tab.

For **entertainment, pop culture, and personals:**

- **Lycos.com.** More a home page than a search engine, Lycos helps you browse as much as search. Click any result, and Lycos deftly brings up the web page, so you can see if it's what you want, but keeps your search results in the left column, so you can easily return to them.
- **Eurekster.com** offers an intriguing twist: personalized search. Your search results are affected by what you and

your friends (the ones who use Eurekster, anyway) have searched for recently. If you and your friends are fans of a new band or TV show, you'll help each other find the best sites.

- **MSN.com Search** offers useful channels to browse, as well as a solid search engine.
- **Yahoo.com** offers numerous popular search categories, such as Real Estate and Personals.

For **shopping in mail-order catalogs:**

- **Catalogs.Google.com** searches 6,000 catalogs and returns pictures from their pages.

For searching **sites in foreign languages:**

- **AltaVista.com,** which offers nice translation tools.

For **when you don't know what term to use:**

- **AskJeeves.com** allows you to type a question. Suppose you want to find information about the current prime minister of Israel but can't remember his name. At AskJeeves, simply type, "Who is the current Israeli prime minister?"

For **phone numbers and addresses:**

- Click the tab for White Pages or for Yellow Pages at **Dogpile.com,** and usually you'll quickly find the right person or business, complete with a map to their location.

For **pictures:**

- **Google.com** offers an easy way to search through 425 million images, using the Image tab on the home page. Close behind are **AltaVista.com** and **Yahoo.com**.

For **videos:**

- **AlltheWeb.com**. Use the Advanced Search under Video to choose streamed or downloadable files and video file format.

For **overall, everyday use,** I like, in this order:

- **Google.com** now conducts 55 percent of all searches on the web, for good reasons.[2] Simple to use, fast, exhaustive, Google usually returns the most relevant results.

- **Mamma.com** stands out because it searches many other engines but returns only the best results. I like getting only a few dozen, highly relevant results.

- **Wisenut.com**'s Sneak-a-Peek feature allows you to open a web page while in the results list so you can see if it's what you want.

- **Teoma.com** offers a simple design with bonus features. Next to your results, you get suggestions on how to narrow your search. For example, search on *"Super Bowl"* and you get six suggestions, including Super Bowl History and Super Bowl Tickets. Below those suggestions, Teoma also gives "collection websites" that may be a mother lode on the topic you searched for. For my search on *"Super Bowl,"* the ten sites listed include www.superbowlhotelrooms.com.

I suggest you bookmark your two favorite search engines so you can quickly return to them. (To bookmark in Outlook, select Favorites ➜ Add to Favorites.) Even better, Google, AltaVista, AskJeeves, and other search engines allow you to add their search box to your browser's toolbar, so you don't even have to visit the site to start searching. I love this. (To add this feature, go to the particular site. At Google.com, for example, click on Services and Tools, then scroll down and click on Google Toolbar.)

2. Add and arrange words to make your search as specific as possible.

Add words to make your search as specific as possible. For example, don't search on *meatloaf* when you really want *meatloaf recipes;* instead of typing *information overload,* key in *surviving information overload.*

Use precise wording. If you're looking for information on scleroderma, type *scleroderma* rather than *skin diseases* or *autoimmune conditions.*

Arrange words in order from most important to least important. Better than *small Midwest colleges* is *colleges Midwest small.*

Avoid common words, since search engines throw those words out anyway. For example, when I searched on *Kevin A. Miller,* the search engine threw out *A* since the word is so common. That meant I got results for Kevin F. Miller and for Kevin Doolittle and Lauren Miller. The solution to this problem is point 3, which in my opinion would help web searchers more than any other.

3. Use quotation marks around phrases.

Instead of typing *Kevin A. Miller,* enter *"Kevin A. Miller,"* and the search engine will return only web pages that include that exact phrase, with the words in that order. Thus, quotation marks usually narrow your search to what you're actually seeking. For example, if I search on *Cornerstone Festival,* I get 59,000 results, but if I add quotation marks and search on *"Cornerstone Festival,"* a summer rock-music event, I get only 4,710.

Quotation marks make it possible to quickly find common information.

To find a **residential phone number,** type *"the person's name" "their city, state abbreviation."* (In Google, add *rphonebook:* at the beginning.)

To find a **commercial phone number,** type *"the company's name" "contact us".* (Or in Google, *bphonebook: "the company's name".*)

To find **directions,** type in *"the address of your destination".* Google gives you two links (one from Yahoo! Maps and the other from MapQuest) so you can quickly get a map of that location. The map pages also contain links for driving directions.

To find the **best price on a product,** type *"the model name and number" "price comparison."*

These first three principles—the right search engine, precise wording, and quotation marks—work together well. *PC* magazine gives a good example:

"Bill and Melinda Gates recently had a baby girl, and you want to find out the baby's name. Lycos and Yahoo! are good sites to use for news searches, because they carry breaking stories from newswire services. *"Bill and Melinda Gates" baby* retrieves pages that are about the Bill and Melinda Gates Foundation and babies in general, so you need to add more definitive terms. If you refine the search to *"Bill and Melinda Gates" daughter,* the first five results are announcements about the new Gates baby."[3]

🖰 *4. Use operators and wildcards.*

Many people search happily without this principle, but if you search the web frequently, take ten minutes to learn it well. Your investment of ten minutes will be amply rewarded.

To make your search exact, **use operators,** which are symbols, or words in capital letters, that tell the search engine what to do and what not to do. Search engines assume the operator *AND* between words. That means they return results that include all the words you typed. For example, *ice hockey* will return only pages that have both the word *ice* and the word *hockey* in them. You won't get pages that have only the word *ice* somewhere, as in Ben and Jerry's ice cream.

The operator *OR* tells the search engine to find pages with *any* of the words you typed. This comes in handy when a word has synonyms and you don't care which word you find. For example, type *turkey AND dressing OR stuffing*. That will return pages with *turkey* and *dressing;* you'll also get pages with *turkey* and *stuffing*.

The operator *NOT,* usually expressed as a minus sign (–), excludes words you don't want. For example, in the earlier example about the Gateses' baby, you could type *"Bill and Melinda Gates" baby – Foundation* to make sure you don't get any pages about the Gates Foundation.

Use a wildcard symbol, usually an asterisk (*), when you need to pull up all forms of a word. For example, *theat** will return theater, theatre, and theatrical. Typing *color** will return colors, coloring, coloration (and Colorado, which you probably don't want; to solve that, type *color* – Colorado*).

Few people will need to search by URL, link, or domain, but should you, see the clear guidelines at SearchEngineWatch.com: http://www.searchenginewatch.com/facts/article.php/2155981.

 5. *When general search engines don't work, try directories, specific sites, or librarians.*

Now you know how to conduct word searches well. But sometimes general search engines still don't yield what you need.

Try the Directory tab. In Google, if your search yields too many results, click the Directory tab at the top of your search results page. This will return websites that focus on your topic and will greatly reduce the number of results. For example, a search on *"Ellen DeGeneres"* yielded 141,000 results. A click on the Directory tab then narrowed that number to 359.

Check out specialized websites for your topic. For example, here are two dozen information sites I've used, in alphabetical order by topic.

Bible: Bible Gateway (http://bible.gospelcom.net). You can search easily by word or Bible verse. Blue Letter Bible (http://blueletterbible.org) adds study tools, maps, hymns, and devotionals.

Books: Amazon.com, of course, or for rare books, Bookfinder.com. And remember that Amazon allows you to search the complete text of 120,000 books.

Business: CEO Express (http://www.ceoexpress.com), a nice portal for business sites.

Cars: Edmunds.com.

Christianity: For current information, Christianity-Today.com, and for classic reading, Christian Classics Ethereal Library (http://www.ccel.org/).

Dictionaries: Bartleby.com outdoes Dictionary.com.

Facts: RefDesk.com calls itself "the single best source for facts" on the Net, and it just might be. If you still don't find what you're looking for, check Library Spot (http://www.libraryspot.com), a portal to virtually any information a library contains.

Health: With nearly 20,000 health websites, many of which offer unproven information, I stay with MayoClinic.com.

Ideas: To stay fresh on the world of ideas, check out Arts and Letters Daily (http://www.aldaily.com/).

Maps: MapQuest.com or MSN Maps and Directions, which offers the nice LineDrive feature (http://maps.msn.com).

Movies: For the content and quality of a specific movie, I like Screenit.com (though it loads slowly). To research actors, directors, and the film industry, choose imdb.com.

Myths and hoaxes: Is that story going around the Net really true? http://www.snopes2.com will know.

Phone numbers: SuperPages.com.

Pictures: The images directory in Google makes finding pictures a snap. Go to http://www.google.com and click on the Images tab.

Sports: Espn.com tops cnnsi.com, in my opinion.

Weather: weather.com.

Call a librarian. Still stumped?

Remember, the web isn't the only way to find information, and often it's not the best way. Writes Richard Saul Wurman: "The highest-tech choice isn't always the most efficient, although sometimes the dazzle blinds us to more dowdy, but perhaps speedier solutions, like the old-fashioned reference librarian. Librarians find information for a living. If you need to know something specific, you can get an answer from a librarian before you can make your way through thousands of responses to a search engine query."[4]

QUESTIONS TO APPLY

- Which of the principles presented in this chapter would help me the most? Why?

- What's the phone number of my nearest reference librarian?

QUOTES TO TAKE WITH YOU

" Our task is not to bring order out of chaos, but to get work done in the midst of chaos.

—*George Peabody*

" Fanaticism consists of redoubling your efforts when you have forgotten your aim.

—*George Santayana*

chapter 8

HOW TO HANDLE VOICE MAIL, JUNK MAIL, AND MAGAZINES

A strategy for the stacks

Read this chapter if:

❑ You have a pile of magazines at work or home.

❑ It takes a while to sort all the junk mail you get.

❑ You find it hard to return voice-mail messages promptly.

Pity your poor mail carriers. Their shoulders must burn under the mailbag strap as they haul each day's mail to your desk. On a recent workday, chosen at random, my mail drop included:

- A brochure promising (for only $1,495) an "intensive, hands-on workshop" from which you will "go back to your office with a complete solution-oriented plan."
- A four-page flyer (see the metallic inks shine!) pointing me to a website that will give me "innovation, perspective, and impact."

- An issue of *U.S. News & World Report* from three months ago. (My name wasn't near the top of the routing slip.)
- A packet of six book reviews, which left me feeling vaguely guilty about all the great books I should be reading but haven't read and probably won't read.
- A promotion for blacktopping and seal-coating—even though I don't make decisions about facilities and never have.
- Three other magazines, one or two of which I really should read.
- An interoffice memo telling me which people would be out of the office on certain days.

I could keep going, but your pile may be higher than mine. Here are some strategies I've found helpful for lowering the stacks.

MAGAZINES

In a classic episode of the original *Star Trek*, "The Trouble with Tribbles," an intergalactic trader named Cyrano Jones gives Lieutenant Uhura a small, furry creature called a tribble. No one knows that tribbles multiply faster than rabbits—but the crew soon finds out. When Captain Kirk sits in his chair on the bridge and lands on a tribble, he commands Uhura to get all tribbles off the *Enterprise.* Too late: the tribbles have spread through the ship's air vents and have even infested bins of grain in a nearby space station. When Kirk opens an overhead storage bin, tribbles shower him. Then Spock calculates how many tribbles must exist on the space station, if you assume each tribble has a litter of ten baby tribbles, every twelve hours, over a period of three days. The answer: what started as one tribble has turned into 1,771,561 tribbles.[1]

Just as Uhura loves tribbles, I love magazines—for seventeen years I've worked for a magazine publisher—but both tribbles and magazines multiply rapidly. One medical doctor did a Spock-like calculation and came up with these frightening numbers: "In one year, 230 journals, 3,200 journal articles, and 50,000 pages of material came across my desk."[2]

If you have too many magazines on your desk or coffee table, what can you do?

🗐 *Pitch the pile.*

Unlike the crew on the *Enterprise*, we can't ask Scotty to beam the multiplying mass onto a nearby Klingon ship. But we can do something similar: we can pitch the pile.

Dr. Marc Ringel says, "One of the healthiest things you can do, when faced by an enormous, guilt-provoking pile of journals, is to throw them all out and start keeping up again from scratch. The consequences on your career of missing several months of journal articles will be unmeasurable, while the positive effects on your mental health may be considerable."[3]

Go ahead, grab that big stack of unread and never-to-be-read magazines and give them the heave-ho.

If you can't bear that thought, then do what one of my friends does: "I put it all in a sack in my closet by my shoes. Then, when I just can't stand it eighteen months later, when I finally sort through what was once urgent and impending material, it's surprising how much of it didn't actually need my attention after all and can simply be thrown away."

🗐 *Choose the two or three most important or enjoyable publications you receive and cancel your subscriptions to the rest.*

I asked Jim, who leads an important nonprofit agency, "What has helped you deal with the information in your life?"

Jim said, "I decided to be more ruthless in what I read. I've cut down subscriptions to only about three periodicals. I convince myself not to be *so* interested in everything."

An information services director named Mike was receiving twenty technology publications per week. As Richard Swenson reports, Mike said, "'It was causing me to be frantic. I saw technology moving so fast, at least on paper, and I couldn't keep up with it.' So he canceled all but two of the subscriptions. 'I wanted everything to stop so I had time to digest it and see how it fit into our organization.'"[4]

📄 *Sign up for online alerts in your key areas of interest.*

An entrepreneur who is a friend of mine used to read thirteen magazines and newspapers and has now cut way back. "But one thing I use now," she says, "are the trackers that many periodicals provide online to alert you to stories of interest. I provide key words to, say, the *New York Times* on subjects of interest, which I try to keep very specific. Then when I receive an alert, I know it's probably something I'd be interested to read." (The *New York Times* tracker allows you to track up to ten subjects at a time. To subscribe, for $19.95 per year, go to http://www.nytimes.com and in the left column, under Member Center, click on News Tracker. For a free alternative, try Google: http://www.google.com/newsalerts.)

Or, if you prefer to limit email but still want targeted information, customize a home page at Yahoo! or Excite.

📄 *Reschedule your magazine reading to down times.*

The pastor of a large church writes, "I'm cautious with periodicals. They can consume a great deal of time, piling up and burying me in a truckload of guilt. So I scan periodicals, occasionally using the last half hour at the office to get through the accumulated stack."[5]

By scheduling magazine reading for down times, it becomes an enjoyable dessert at the end of a day, and it ensures that the majority of the day is spent on higher priorities.

JUNK MAIL

If you have a colleague who opens mail for you, count yourself blessed. But many, probably most, knowledge workers open their own mail. Here are a few time-saving tips:

Open your mail standing up.

Though embarrassingly simple, this is my favorite strategy for handling junk mail. I now open mail while standing at a file cabinet, near a paper-recycling bin. Standing up ensures I don't start leisurely reading a magazine or catalog. (If I see an article I want to read, I tag it with a Post-it for later.) But most things get immediately passed to (a) a basket for outgoing mail or (b) the recycling bin.

Try standing while you sort your mail. At first it may seem odd, but it markedly reduces your mail-handling time.

Toss without reading.

My friend Mark, a skilled magazine editor, confesses, "One bit of advice that has helped an obsessive reader like me: don't even open junk mail. Just toss it."

I, too, count myself an obsessive reader. At a restaurant dinner one night, my wife caught me reading the bottom of the coffee cup. How else could I know where it was made? But when I started Mark's practice of tossing junk mail without opening it, I cut my processing time in half.

Only handle it once.

Says a marketer and mother: "My goal is to touch a piece of mail only once to put it in the right spot: trash, bill to pay, something to save, something to respond to. Of course, I'm not always good about this, but otherwise the clutter becomes unbearable after a short time."

Remove your home address from marketing lists.

To spend less time handling junk mail, you need to work mostly on the supply side, removing your name from various lists. Doing this won't eliminate junk mail but will reduce it.

For general **direct mail,** contact the Direct Marketing Association's Mail Preference Service (MPS). Either send a letter to Mail Preference Service, P.O. Box 643, Carmel, NY 10512, or register online, which costs five dollars, at http://www.dmacon sumers.org/cgi/offmailinglistdave. Before you register with the MPS, be sure you really want to stop most reputable direct mail. If you like seeing offers, request removal only from individual companies' lists, by calling each company's toll-free number.

Catalogs also act like tribbles, because as soon as you buy from one catalog house, your name will be rented by other companies, and you'll be sent many more catalogs. To remove your name from a cooperative database of catalog customers, write to Abacus, P.O. Box 1478, Broomfield, CO 80038, or call 1-800-518-4453.[6]

To get out of **city directories,** which may be used by local marketers, write to the two largest creators of these: (1) Haines and Company, Inc., Criss-Cross Directory, Attn: Director of Data Processing, 8050 Freedom Ave. N.W., North Canton, OH 44720; and (2) Equifax, Attn: List Suppression File, 26955 Northwestern Hwy., South Field, MI 48034, 1-800-873-7655.[7]

To block many **credit card offers,** call 1-888-5-OPTOUT. This removes your address from the rental lists of four large companies that provide consumer credit reports.[8]

📰 *Reduce your junk mail at work.*

This is difficult to do. No wonder a study of a Seattle company showed "the mailroom staff was spending 25 percent of its time sorting Standard Class (formerly Third Class) advertising mail."[9] Obviously, this wastes time and money.

You can help to reduce your junk mail in two ways. First, you can give names of former employees to Red Flag, so those names get removed from direct mail lists. (Read more at http://www.redflagservices.com/employer/employer.html.) Second, you can ask Dun and Bradstreet to remove your company from its business marketing lists. Call 1-800-333-0505 or email http://custserv@dnb.com.[10]

VOICE MAIL

Think back, far back, to those thrilling days of yesteryear, when if you stepped away from your phone, someone else took a message for you on the ubiquitous pink slip that read While You Were Out. This system meant that the message was always kept short and also that you could quickly flip through the messages and arrange them in order of importance. Now with voice mail, many messages run long, and there's no easy way to sort them by priority. This limitation requires certain strategies to reduce voice mail.

📰 *Supercharge your voice-mail message.*

Go beyond the generic voice-mail message to explain (a) when you'll be able to return the call and (b) what the caller can do till then. One man I know says on his voice mail: "I return calls Monday through Thursday." This tells me that if I'm calling on Friday, I shouldn't expect to hear back till Monday. The information is helpful, and the voice mail also gives me a number to call in case of emergencies.

📄 *Choose carefully to whom you give your number, and change your number periodically.*

As with junk mail, to reduce junk phone calls, reduce the number of people who have your number. Everyone's familiar with unlisted numbers, caller ID, and other strategies. But marketers seek phone numbers like missiles seek heat.

Dean, a sales rep in the Washington, D.C., area, says, "In every store I go into now, the clerk asks, 'Can I have your phone number?'

"I say, 'No, I don't want calls.'

"The clerk replies, 'Oh, we never call anyone.'

"'Then you don't need my phone number, do you?'"

Another leader changes his cell phone number every year. Even though he gives his cell number only to key people, it has a way of being passed on to others, so each year he starts fresh.

📄 *Set a time when you will not answer your phone.*

Richard Carlson writes, "I was once in the office of a manager when the phone rang. Immediately, he bellowed, 'That darn phone never stops ringing.' He then proceeded to pick it up and engage in a fifteen-minute conversation while I waited. When he finally hung up, he looked exhausted and frustrated. He apologized as the phone rang once again. He later confessed that he was having a great deal of trouble completing his tasks because of the volume of calls he was responding to. At some point I asked him, 'Have you ever considered having a certain period of time when you simply don't answer the phone?' He looked at me with a puzzled look on his face and said, 'As a matter of fact, no.' It turned out that this simple suggestion helped him not only to relax, but to get more work done as well. Like many people, he didn't need hours of uninterrupted time, but he did need some!"[11]

As Carlson points out, this idea offers a fringe benefit: when *you* return the call, you can say, "I can't talk long but really wanted to get back to you soon," and you can shorten the call, if necessary.

Consider the following ideas:

- Turn off the ringer for a brief time. If you can't do that during the workday, then do so before or after work, so you can have a few minutes of peace and quiet. One woman's job requires her to be on call. "Sometimes, I take the battery out of my beeper for a half hour," she confesses. "I just need a break from constantly being accessible."

- Forward your calls to voice mail or to a friend who agrees to cover for a time (and maybe you return the favor).

- If you're really buried by a mission-critical project, ask a friend to help answer the phone. One woman who worked for a Big Five accounting firm remembers when she took on a new project: "My phone was ringing nonstop. Probably the best thing I did in the heat of this project was to ask a friend to sit in and answer my phone to help me keep on track. She was able to summarize my messages for me and return those calls when I was able to get answers for her. Life doesn't always afford that luxury, but it helped me concentrate on what is critical."[12]

Sometimes we could, or even should, turn off the phone, but we fear being inaccessible. Overcome that fear. Quentin Schultze, author of *Habits of the High-Tech Heart*, reports what happened one Sunday morning at a church in Maine. During the pastor's sermon, "a cell phone went off ringing. Of course, that unnerved everybody, but then it went off a second time.

About that time, people were focusing on whose phone it is. Then it rang a third time, and everybody's wondering what's going to happen. What happened is that a guy answered the phone right in the middle of the service and carries on a conversation that's not very important at all. The pastor's waiting for him to finish. The guy finishes the conversation, and then the pastor carries on."[13]

▤ *Remove your phone number from online phonebooks.*
Here's how to do that in four of the most popular services:

Google: fill in the form at http://www.google.com/help/pbremoval.html. For a business number, mail a signed request on company letterhead to Google Phonebook Removal, 2400 Bayshore Parkway, Mountain View, CA 94043. Google states, "Include a phone number at which you can be reached so that we may verify your phonebook removal request."

Smartpages.com: Email http://complaints@infousa.com with the listing exactly as it displays on the site.

Switchboard.com: Fill out the form at (and sorry they give such a long URL): http://www.switchboard.com/bin/cgiqa.dll?LNK=24:3&MEM=1&FUNC=DELETE.

Whitepages.com: "E-mail your full name, phone number and address exactly as they appear in our directory listings, as well as your daytime phone number, to remove@whitepages.com."

▤ *Register your home or cell phone number with the National Do Not Call Registry.*
In June 2003, the U.S. government launched the National Do Not Call Registry, a service that allows consumers to list phone numbers that most telemarketers may not call. The registry made headlines when in its first four days, consumers listed

more than 10 million of their home or cell phone numbers.[14] To register is free and simple; go to http://www.DoNotCall.gov, or call 1-888-382-1222. Your request will take effect in three months and will block most telemarketing calls for five years.

Of course, if none of the above strategies works to reduce your magazines, junk mail, and voice mail, you can always take the humorous advice of my friend Jim Berkley: "It doesn't hurt to change jobs now and then. Suddenly, the stream of information is cut short, and it takes a while for the persistent, probing mass of information to find me again— hidden in a swamp somewhere, breathing out of a straw."[15]

QUESTIONS TO APPLY

- Which of these three—magazines, junk mail, or voice mail—is the greatest challenge for me?

- What one action could I take to lighten my load in that area?

QUOTES TO TAKE WITH YOU

It's just as foolish to use every minute for activity as it is to spend every nickel you've got.

—Fred Smith[16]

Lord, I shall be very busy this day. I may forget Thee, but do not Thou forget me.

—Sir Jacob Astley

chapter 9

HOW TO ORGANIZE, FILE, AND STORE INFORMATION

It's not about neatness;
it's about quick retrieval and simplicity

Read this chapter if:

❑ You spend more time than you want to looking for things.

❑ While working on a project, you get distracted by the stacks in your office.

Take a look at your desk. Scan the work sitting on it: stacks of papers, file folders, reports, and letters. How long would it take you to finish that work?

If you're like the average desk worker, you'd have to work thirty-six hours to clear your desk. Meanwhile, you're spending three hours a week just sorting through it.[1]

Computers were supposed to decrease the amount of paper in your office—remember the utopian dreams of the paperless office?—but computers have actually greatly increased paper consumption. Why? Because they give you access to many more documents, some of which you need to print; paper is easier to read and flip through. And when working in a group, paper is still the best way to quickly distribute information. No wonder personal paper consumption tripled between 1980 and 1990.[2]

Meanwhile, today's office, despite its computer and growing stacks of paper, is shrinking. The *Chicago Tribune* reports: "The average office space per person . . . dropped from 410 square feet per person in 1997 to 347 square feet in 2002. . . . Standard offices for executives 'used to be 250 square feet, and now range from 150 to 180 square feet.'"[3]

To handle more paper in less space, we need new ways to organize, file, and store information.

But before we set to work, let's remember our goal.

📁 *Don't worry about orderliness; the goal is to be organized.*

I once worked with a woman named Gloria. If you happened into Gloria's office, you had to stand, because the lone chair overflowed with books and papers, some about to fall. You couldn't enter much past the doorway, in fact, because more stacks, some three feet high, lined the walls, leaving just enough room for Gloria to skinny back to her desk chair. I couldn't determine the color of Gloria's desk, because the surface lay buried beneath high stacks of jumbled paper: manuscripts, books in galley form, paperback books, letters, file folders, and old newspapers. Some stacks stood four inches high, some eight, some twenty-four.

I secretly looked down on Gloria. *Her desk looks like the skyline of Chicago. If one stack tips, all the rest will fall, like dominoes, and Gloria will lie crushed under the heap.*

One day I couldn't find an article, and I thought Gloria had it. *This will be futile,* I said to myself, but I went and stood in Gloria's doorway and asked, "Have you seen that article?" Gloria nodded. She quickly eyed her stacks, zoomed in on the second stack from the left, lifted the top four inches of the pile, and—voilà!—pulled out the article.

"Uh, thank you," I said, not quite believing what I had seen. No file folders, no color codes, no alphabetical order, yet Gloria had put her fingers on the article faster than I could.

Yeah, she was just lucky with that particular article, I decided. But in weeks to come, I saw Gloria do the same thing every time I asked her for something. I finally realized, *Gloria's system beats mine. She may not be orderly, but she is organized.*

Business executive Fred Smith writes, "It's important to know the difference between orderliness and organization. People who are too fastidious turn orderliness into an end rather than a means—and that takes a lot of time. It's much more important to be organized. . . . A certain amount of orderliness is necessary, of course, but as long as I know how to do my job effectively, I'm organized—and no amount of orderliness will help."[4]

This distinction matters. Our goal is not a neat desk; it's to know where to find things. Our goal is not a clean office; it's to be able to concentrate.

If you can find what you need to find (in a reasonable period of time), it doesn't matter how messy your office is. If you can focus on your most important tasks, it doesn't matter how cluttered your office is. Don't worry about the stacks. Instead, ask yourself:

1. Can I find what I need to find in a reasonable period of time?
2. Am I able to focus on what most needs to be done?

If you answered yes to both questions, skip this chapter. If you answered no to one or both questions, read on.

📁 *Friendly Tip 1: Make a date with your piles.*

Cleaning never just happens. You have to schedule an hour, a morning, or a full day to make it happen. Says Harriet Schlechter, who heads the Miracle Worker Organizing Service, "If you don't commit blocks of time to the job, it won't get done. After an initial session, you'll have an idea of how long the job will take. From there, schedule several shorter clean-up sessions rather than one marathon to keep yourself moving forward."[5]

My company holds an annual Clean-Up Day on a Friday in June. Employees wear grubby clothes to work and spend the morning sorting, organizing, cleaning, and throwing out. Usually, on a single Clean-Up Day, our modest-sized company fills two giant dumpsters with paper to be recycled. On the recent Clean-Up Day, I alone threw out five bins of old files and unnecessary paper, each bin the size of a giant laundry basket.

To make the day more appealing, the company pays for a barbecue lunch on the lawn. (For that reason, Clean-Up Day got listed on a corporate sheet of employee *benefits*, a fact worthy of a *Dilbert* cartoon.) But though I used to mildly resent Clean-Up Day, I've come to appreciate its genius. Clean-Up Day works, because everyone is cleaning, so you don't feel odd for doing it alone. Clean-Up Day forces me to stop and gain control of my office, and that forced day makes me more efficient for the next 364 days.

So make a date with your piles. If you're like me, you'll find that investing one morning per year in cleaning your office will yield high returns.

📁 *Friendly Tip 2: Do initial pile biopsies.*

Harriet Schlechter recommends, "Sample all your stacks with a quick once-over to see what categories you can make. Most people will need 6 to 12 categories."[6]

I took Harriet's advice, and I found she accurately estimated the number of categories I needed. Here are the categories I came up with, though your list will probably read differently, which is fine:

1. Projects Our Team Is Working On
2. Staff I Supervise
3. Workshops or Seminars I Have Presented or Might Someday
4. Corporate Committees I Serve On
5. Stuff I Need for General Meetings Coming Up
6. Stuff I Need for Employee Meetings Coming Up
7. Phone Calls I Need to Make
8. Stuff for Phone Calls I Made but Haven't Heard Back from the Other Person Yet
9. Tasks I Really Need to Do Right Now, No Kidding
10. Tasks I Need to Do Right After That

No matter what categories you come up with, the point is simple: don't build an elaborate filing system that doesn't fit how you actually work. Start by finding out how you are working now. Don't worry if your current system seems chaotic or inconsistent. You'll find it much easier to get organized if you work with categories that seem natural to you.

📁 *Friendly Tip 3: Consolidate your filing categories.*

For example, did I really need one filing category for Staff I Supervise and a separate filing category for Stuff I Need for Employee Meetings Coming Up? No. I could, and did, put everything into one staff file, organized alphabetically by employee name.

Then I asked myself, *Do I need separate files for Projects Our Team Is Working On and Corporate Committees I Serve On?*

I decided I didn't. They may be two different types of activity, but they can be filed together without any loss.

By making decisions like these, I was able to reduce my filing categories from ten to six, which made my files easier to maintain and to access.

As you settle on your filing categories, here's some helpful advice from Harriet Schlechter: "The files you use most often should be most accessible and easily identifiable. It's most helpful to color-code these files." And "Avoid a general pile or file marked 'urgent' or 'pending'—you'll have to spend 15 minutes looking through it just to figure out what you have to do."[7]

📁 *Friendly Tip 4: Leave visible only what you are working on at the moment.*

The problem with not filing enough is that soon too many papers surround me, each calling out, "Do me! Answer me! Finish me!" I get distracted and feel overwhelmed. Says Fred Smith, "When I diet, I don't leave food lying around the house to tantalize me. Unfinished work tempts me, makes me want to look at it, pick it up, finish it. I feel guilty about it. So ... I must remove from sight the intimidating stuff I'm not going to use."[8]

But if I decide to clear my desk, the problem is that, as my friend Jeanne explains, "Once things are in a file, it's easy to forget that these things exist and need to be done."

So I try to file as much as I can but leave visible only the things I am working on right now. One mom describes her system: "I take my to-do papers and stand them vertically in a decorative basket. This makes it easy to flip through them, but the papers are still out in sight to remind me they need to be done."

📂 *Friendly Tip 5: As much as possible, handle things only once.*
What we're all tempted to do, but must resist, is to pick up and half read a memo or article and then set it down, to finish later. When a magazine or brochure comes, either read it or toss it. When a memo comes, read it and file it or toss it. Decide now, so you don't have to touch the paper again.

Whenever you pick up a piece of paper, you have only four options, which Stephanie Winston describes in *The Organized Executive:* Toss, Refer, Act, or File. Thus, she calls her method the TRAF Technique. Here's how it works:

Toss:	Do you need this now or later? If not ...	→	Trash can
Refer:	Can a secretary handle this? Would this be better suited for a coworker?	→	Outbox
Act:	Is this something you alone must read, answer, review?	→	To-do box or Reading pile
File:	Will you need this later?	→	Files[9]

The TRAF Technique helps me handle most papers only once. Ahhh.

📂 *Friendly Tip 6: Ask yourself, "Does anyone else keep this information?"*
Yes, much information must be stored, but does it all have to be stored by you? Maybe not.

I used to keep copies of our contracts with book publishers. I finally realized that if I really needed to see a contract, I could ask the person who keeps all our contracts on file. I no longer bother to keep an extra.

The same applies to marketing plans. Other people prepared the plans and showed them to me. I kept a copy of each plan. Did this make sense, when on the rare times I needed to refer to a marketing plan, I could simply walk down the hall and ask for one?

By trusting others more, I significantly shrink the amount of paper I need to organize, file, and store.

🗁 *Friendly Tip 7: Store all of your text files in one software program.*

Since Microsoft Office contains four or five programs, I can easily store some files in Word, some in Outlook. The downside of this: many times I can't find a file because I don't know which program I stored it in. How many times have you had documents for the same project filed in different programs? Maybe one exists in Word and the other in an email subfolder in Outlook.

I find it less confusing to keep all my text files in Word. When an email arrives that I want to keep, I click File ➜ Save As and save the email in the appropriate project's folder in Word. Otherwise I delete the email and never, ever look at it again.

Some people, especially heavy email users, file email in folders and subfolders in Outlook. If this works for you, great. You'll get no complaint from me. But neither will you convince me to adopt your system, because (a) I like to have all text files, whether .doc or .eml or .txt. or .html, in one folder, and Word makes that easier; (b) if I need to format the content later, I prefer to use Word's more powerful formatting tools; and (c) I find the folders in Outlook harder to navigate than Word's.

By the way, if I have a file on my computer, I do not keep a paper copy. If the file exists in one place, I don't need it in another. Therefore, the only things that belong in my paper files are documents someone else created or handwritten notes. (The foregoing assumes your computer files are backed up regularly.)

📁 *Friendly Tip 8: Give computer files long, clear, and boring names.*

Once you've filled eight gigabytes of hard drive, mostly with Word files, you realize you can no longer name files with short, oft-used names like Agenda, Report, or Memo. If you do, you'll search long and hard for the precise file you need. Better to name the file something long, clear, and boring, such as Meeting Notes with John LaRue and Anita Lopez July 4.

If I'm searching for a file in Word, and I still can't tell if a certain file is the one I want, I use the Preview feature. In the Open dialog box (File→Open, or Ctrl + O), there's an icon for Views in the upper-right-hand corner. Click the small down arrow next to that icon and drag down to Preview. This opens a pane that shows you what's in each file before you open it.

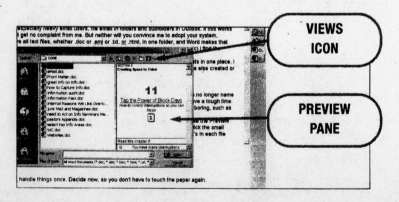

If I still can't find a file on my computer, I use Windows'
Search feature (Start→Search→For files or folders; or the
Windows key + F). Some people avoid the Search feature
because, as set by default, it searches your entire hard drive,
which takes a long time. But the Search moves quickly when
you narrow it to the folders where your file probably lies.
Here's how to narrow your search:

1. In the left-hand column, under Look in:, click the
   down arrow and drag down to Browse. The Browse
   dialog box will open up.
2. In the Browse dialog box, find the program or folder
   where you think your file probably exists. Click OK.

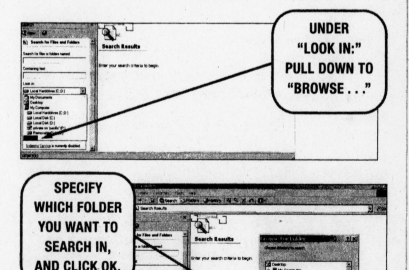

UNDER
"LOOK IN:"
PULL DOWN TO
"BROWSE . . ."

SPECIFY
WHICH FOLDER
YOU WANT TO
SEARCH IN,
AND CLICK OK.

If you now feel more overwhelmed than when you began this chapter, I have failed. For the heart of this chapter beats with wonderfully freeing principles, which bear repeating:

- Don't worry about orderliness, as long as you're organized. The goal is not a neat desk; it's to find what you need in a reasonable period of time.
- Build your filing system on the way you already work, no matter how chaotic or inconsistent it seems. You don't have to build an elaborate filing system that doesn't fit how you work.
- You may not have to file as much information as you think you do. Often someone else is required to keep that information, and you can request it whenever you need it.

QUESTIONS TO APPLY

- Which of this chapter's closing three principles do I find most helpful? Why?

- When could I make a date with my piles?

QUOTES TO TAKE WITH YOU

" I would not give a fig for the simplicity this side of complexity, but I would give my life for the simplicity on the other side of complexity.
—*Oliver Wendell Holmes*

" Dear God, I find it so easy to try to be the one in charge. I find it so painful to realize that I am not the one in control.
—*Dick Rasanen*

part 3

CREATING
Space to Think
Finding an oasis amid the overload

chapter 10

TAP THE POWER OF BLOCK DAYS
How to control interruptions so you can focus

Read this chapter if:

- ❏ You have many interruptions at work.

- ❏ Projects that require chunks of time are not getting done.

- ❏ You feel like you have no time to think.

Four years ago, my work was moving me into a new role, and I felt uncertain about my ability to adjust. The department had grown (from two people to eight people in just three years), and I was shifting from leading doers to leading leaders. *What should I do to effectively lead leaders?* I wondered. *What has to change in my daily work patterns?*

I not only felt uncertain; I felt frustrated. The pace of my work had accelerated, and I could no longer find time to read for professional growth. I couldn't remember the last time I'd read an important article or a chapter from a book.

Plus, I had no time to write, which ranks as one of the most enjoyable parts of my job. My days were crammed with meetings, memos, budgets, and problems. Writing for two uninterrupted hours had become a luxury I could not afford.

About this time, a friend named Bill began working as a personal coach, and he offered to help me.

I had read about "personal coaches," consultants who work one-on-one with executives and other leaders to increase their effectiveness. But I had never considered trying one. I think the name "personal coach" smacked of "personal trainer," a status symbol for Hollywood stars.

Still, my uncertainty and frustration were not going away; they were growing. So not knowing what to expect, I told Bill yes.

In his introductory email, Bill asked four questions, which I had to answer at our first meeting:

1. What are the 1–3 most important things you'd like to accomplish as we work together over the next 90 days? Please be very specific.
2. What, if anything, is likely to get in the way or prevent you from accomplishing any of these things?
3. What's the most important thing you need from me as we work on these objectives?
4. How will you know your investment in coaching has been worthwhile?[1]

During our first meeting (a phone call that lasted thirty to forty-five minutes, placed by me), I explained my answer to Bill's first question. "I'm spending more and more time in meetings," I said, "and I'm not getting time to do some valuable but less urgent tasks. I don't have time to write, to read for personal and professional growth, to plan, to just plain think. I'm frustrated, and I feel I have no control over my schedule."

Bill asked, "Have you ever thought about block days?"

"What's a block day?"

Bill explained how to carve blocks of time in my calendar, setting aside either a day or half a day for each block. These blocks cannot be used for meetings, for answering email, for handling any routine work. Instead, these blocks must be devoted to personal development, professional growth, and major projects I can't get to during my usual (out-of-control) days.

"I've heard of something similar and even tried it for a while," I said. "But I always slip back into my jammed routine."

So Bill asked a few questions: "How far ahead do you schedule your block days? Where do you spend your block days?" He quickly determined I was going about block days the wrong way. Then he gave me three suggestions that took me to a new level.

"First, block days farther ahead. Do that now for the entire year.

"Then, treat those block days as iron-clad commitments. If an emergency comes up, don't skip your block day; move it to another spot in the calendar." Bill solemnly advised me: "You can move a block, but never remove a block.

"Finally," Bill suggested, "Spend your block days outside the office, if you can, where you'll focus without interruptions. Get off-site. Make sure it's a pleasant place you will enjoy going to."

Hmmm. I didn't like the idea of spending days out of the office. Sure, it sounded nice, but wouldn't my staff resent it when they needed me but couldn't find me? Would they think I wasn't really working?

THE EXPERIMENT

I tentatively shared the concept with three key people on our team. "So what do you think?" I asked.

"I think it's fine," Phyllis said. "It's really no different than now. Some days you're in meeting after meeting, so even though you're in the office, you're not accessible to us then." The other two nodded and encouraged me to try a few block days. So I said I would schedule three off-site block days and see how they went. I would work someplace no farther away than a fifteen minutes' drive, and they could reach me by cell phone in an emergency.

The following Thursday, I took my laptop to a college library and found a quiet carrel on the second floor. I started working. About forty-five minutes later I checked my watch: I'd been working for almost an hour, and I hadn't had one interruption. I couldn't believe it. But it was true. I couldn't send or receive emails. I couldn't make phone calls (because the library insists on quiet), and short of an emergency, no one would call me. No stacks of undone work called out "Look at me!" The walls of the carrel acted like blinders on a racehorse: they kept me on the track.

By the end of the day, I had finished two major projects, both of which had lain dormant on my desk for ten days (waiting for a chunk of time). I had done essential planning for the department, thinking through priorities and opportunities. *Hey, I am actually looking long-range and thinking beyond the immediate demands,* I realized. I had even read two articles on innovation.

My first full block day surprised me. Though I had accomplished twice as much as on a typical workday, at the end of the day I felt refreshed.

I now view block days as one of my best defenses against information overload. They shelter me from the hail of incoming information and give me space to think.

On my block days, I do four things, every one of which I can't easily complete on a regular workday. Convenient for remembering, they start with the same letter:

1. Projects (essential ones requiring deeper thinking and larger chunks of time)
2. Planning (of my schedule, to-do list, and department priorities)
3. Personal Growth (reading that will help me become more effective)
4. Prayer (for our team's work and relationships)

I think you can see why block days have become one of the most productive and powerful practices in my life. Block days help me gain control over my schedule, over interruptions, over information overload. I calm and clear my mind and regain focus.

One of the hardest-working executives I've ever met wrote this: "I guard two things in life: savings and time alone. I simply must have two days every so often to talk to nobody. Otherwise, I can't stay in control of myself. I can't feel I am directing my life. . . . People lose sight of the fact that relaxation is part of the foundation of one's contribution. How can you do any thinking if you don't spend time alone, unpressured, refreshed?"[2]

MINI-BLOCKS

Whenever I talk about block days, people say or imply, "Must be nice." They ask incredulously, "How can you get away like that?" or say quickly and flatly, "I could never do that."

I understand, because some of them (about 30 percent of knowledge workers, in my informal survey) can't block a day. They work in a job or under a boss or in a corporate culture that won't allow it. They must always be on-site or covering the beeper or working with students.

For these folks, I suggest mini-blocks—chunks of time of one, two, or three hours. During this time, they will let their phone calls go into voice mail. Or they will forward their calls to a willing friend. They may move from their noisy cubicle to a quiet conference room down the hall. But during this mini-block, they will reduce as many interruptions as possible and eliminate incoming information as much as possible so that they can focus and think.

Richard Swenson explains, "The average middle manager in America, according to one study, is interrupted seventy-four times every day. Interruptions are a part of modern life, but with effort, they can be modified. Relocate to a quieter room. Go to the library to work. . . . Have other people take messages for you and return them in a batched fashion. Control the telephone. Turn off the beeper. Employ technologies that block interruptions rather than cause them."[3]

In my role, I can take a full, off-site block day only about once a month, but I take two mini-blocks every week. Mini-blocks pack a punch beyond their size. Most people would become significantly more productive if they could work without interruption for even one or two hours a day. Even a few minutes—minutes!—of quiet can make a difference.

Richard Carlson writes about "one of the most successful CEOs that I've ever met . . . Every day, regardless of how busy he is, he picks a time to enjoy his few minutes of quiet. He realizes that the busier he is, the more it's needed. He jokingly told me, 'My quiet time has made me realize how much idle chatter runs through my mind, mostly nonsense. Clearly, all that noise gets in the way of my being able to see right to the heart of the matter. A few minutes of doing nothing usually cuts through the clutter.'"[4]

I have yet to meet a knowledge worker who couldn't take and benefit from an occasional mini-block.

WHY PEOPLE DON'T TAKE BLOCK DAYS

Now let's talk about that other, much larger group of knowledge workers who could take an entire block day but don't do it. This group includes writers, consultants, professors, pastors, many lawyers, entrepreneurs, some sales people, and others. They have some control over their schedule and some control over where they work. They see that an occasional block day would help them, and they could take one. But they don't.

Why not?

The answer is usually one of the following concerns.

☐ *"I'm needed in the office."* I feel that, too. My absence might cause delay or frustration for others. But I'm not as needed as I might think. As Peter Drucker explains: "We usually tend to overrate rather than underrate our importance and to conclude that far too many things can be done only by ourselves."[5] Plus, if there's a genuine, all-hands-on-deck emergency, I can be reached even on my occasional block day.

☐ *"What will people think?"* This was my strongest initial objection. So I hesitatingly broached the idea with my team.

Surprise! They thought block days were a good idea. That's partly because I explained how my block day would help them: "Sometimes when you want me to review your projects, I don't get them back to you as soon as I'd like to. I don't want to be a bottleneck. If I had an occasional block day, you would get your projects back sooner. Plus, I'm likely to come back from a block day refreshed, with more energy and clearer vision for our work."

I also made the idea more palatable by asking only for an experiment of three block days. After that, we'd stop and evaluate how it was working. (After the trial period, everyone felt fine about it, so my block days continued.)

☐ *"I feel slightly guilty."* Several months after I started to take block days, my coach asked me how they were going.

"I, uh, haven't taken one for a while," I admitted.

"Why not?" Bill asked.

"Well, I don't know. I've been kind of busy."

Bill could tell this was a smoke screen, so he started asking questions. In a few minutes he discovered the real reason: "So you don't think it's okay to take care of yourself."

I paused. "I wouldn't have put it that way, but I guess you're right," I admitted.

"Look," Bill said, "a part of what the company ought to expect from you—even if they do not—is that you are tending to yourself. Some of that tending, not all of it, should legitimately happen on company time. You will be better at your projects, better at your management, more creative. They get their money's worth out of the time you spend." Then Bill read me a quote from Parker Palmer: "Self-care is never a selfish act; it is simply good stewardship of the only gift I have, the gift I was put on earth to offer to others."

That quote began to bore through my thick cranium, and I am starting to see taking a block day not as a selfish act but as a responsible act. I owe it to the people around me to keep myself sharp, focused, productive.

I can't imagine many vocations with more pressing, constant demands than being a mother of young children. But two mothers I know manage to take block half days. Their husbands watch the kids during that time, and the women go to a coffee shop to read, pray, and collect their sanity. Just sitting without interruptions—no kids crying or fighting or needing something—is powerfully healing for them. And when they return home, their children and husbands benefit from the time these moms spent away.

ⓘ *"I'm so busy, I can't afford to be away from work that long."* My friend Eirik works in the competitive and fast-moving pharmaceutical-benefits industry. He describes the environment at his corporate headquarters as "trying to drink from a fire hose." Can someone like him find time to take a block day?

Eirik told me, "There's a common assumption that the quantity of worked hours has risen dramatically. But those polls rely on workers' ability to estimate actual worked hours. When researchers asked people to daily log their actual worked hours, they found that some folks who claimed eighty-hour workweeks were closer to fifty-three hours.

"I have to say this rings true. As I wander the halls, I observe people standing in office doorways discussing with rolled eyes how stressed they are and how overworked they feel. I rarely walk into an office and see somebody engrossed in a project. And the few people like that are the most productive ones, who are actually in the building for no more than forty hours and who display no unusual stress marks."[6]

Yes, we all feel stress, but as Eirik points out, that may come "more from attitude than the actual hours worked." A person who works forty to forty-five hours may actually accomplish much more than someone who works fifty-three hours. The key is to make those hours productive, and a block day greatly helps with that.

 "I just can't get it together." We all struggle with a lack of self-discipline. The best antidote is to have a friend, spouse, or coach periodically ask you, "Are you taking your block

"So I had a couple hours with nuthin' to do,
so I thought I'd drop in and see you."

(Source: © 1986 *Leadership*. Concept: David L. McAllister. Art: Ron Wheeler. Used with permission.)

days?" The second-best antidote is to block days on your calendar far ahead and to live by Bill's dictum, "You can move a block, but never remove a block."

THREE FINAL QUESTIONS

By now you may be convinced that block days could work for you. They could reduce your interruptions, dike the heaving sea of information, and allow you to think, learn, plan, and recalibrate. (But if you're not convinced block days or miniblocks will work for you, that's okay, too; skip ahead to the next chapter.)

If you're ready to experiment with block days, let me address three final questions you may have.

[1] *Does it matter where I hold my block day?* I didn't used to think so, but yes.

My coach would cringe if he knew this, but several times I've tried to hold block days in the office. I thought, *I've got everything I need there, and if I'm in the office, people won't feel I'm gone.* I put a Please Do Not Disturb sign on my office door and closed it. Then I set about the four Ps: Projects, Planning, Personal Growth, and Prayer.

It never worked. Someone would knock on my door. Yes, they saw the sign, they always hasten to explain, but this will only take a minute and it's important; the fate of the free world hangs upon it. Well, okay, they don't actually say the part about the fate of the free world, but they imply it.

Then the phone rings. Even though I don't pick up—I let the call go into voice mail—the ring interrupts me. Then I see a stack of papers on the edge of my desk and realize that some of them require action ASAP.

Before long, I'm back in my usual routine, responding to emergencies and emails and drowning in information and interruption. I can't think, plan, work in depth, or pray.

So forget about doing your block day in the office. You can successfully hold mini-blocks of one or two hours in the office. But if you want an entire day of focus, leave the office behind.

I've also tried holding block days at home. My home is comfortable, requires no extra expenditures, and is quiet since my kids are not home during the day. But at home I see projects that need to be done. *Hmm. That light fixture really needs to be replaced.* Or since I have email access, *I'll just pick up a few emails and answer them quickly; this won't take long.* My block day disintegrates.

Caribou Coffee works well for me. Many people bring laptops there, and it offers legal stimulants—caffeine and chocolate. But I can't work effectively at the coffee shop for more than one or two hours. The furniture gets uncomfortable, and the noise level can run high.

My best locations for block days so far? College libraries. They're quiet. They have power if I want to plug in my laptop, plus water fountains, bathrooms, and a place to get coffee nearby.

Your best place for block days may be something much different and much better than these suggestions. Maybe it's an affordable hotel room: Richard Swenson notes that "overloaded people are checking into local motels just to escape."[7] Whatever you choose, look for a place that helps you think (and for most people, that means it reduces or eliminates interruptions; you can't get news or email there). And make sure it's someplace you enjoy.

In *Thinking for a Change*, John Maxwell writes about his "thinking places": "I believe I often get thoughts because I make it a habit to frequently go to my thinking places. If you want to consistently generate ideas, you need to do the same thing. Find a place where you can think, and plan to capture your thoughts on paper so that you don't lose them. When I found a place to think my thoughts, my thoughts found a place in me."[8]

[i] *What exactly should I do on a block day?* I recommend some combination of the four Ps: Projects, Planning, Personal Growth, and Prayer (assuming that, like me, you are part of the overwhelming majority of Americans who pray). The time spent on each P varies, but generally I allocate this way: Projects, four or five hours; Planning, one and a half hours; Personal Growth, one and a half hours; Prayer, half an hour.

You can allocate your time any way you wish, and you don't have to include all four Ps in one block day. What I do strongly recommend is that during the Projects part of your block day, you work on something central, essential, and core. Don't allow your precious focused time to drift to something tangential or secondary. Devote your block days to what Dale Burke, pastor of First Evangelical Free Church in Fullerton, California, calls your "main thing."

Burke describes this well: "Main things are defined by three characteristics.

"First, my main thing is mission critical, essential to the health and growth of the ministry. It must be done well if the mission is to move forward.

"Second, my main thing is top priority. . . .

"Third, main things grow out of unique abilities. Over time, I have reduced the scope of my responsibilities to focus on my zone of unique abilities. That zone can be found by identifying and concentrating on three areas: God-given gifts, passions, and experiences. The convergence of these three areas is a leader's 'unique ability zone.'"[9]

☐ *How often should I schedule a block day?* The frequency of your block days will depend on how fast the pace is at your job and what your office routine is like. I try to hold one out-of-office block day every month. (Actually, I schedule two and usually end up with one. As soon as I schedule a block day, all the evil forces of inertia work against my taking it.) I also try to hold two in-office mini-blocks every week. These act as a pressure-release valve for me.

Whatever number of block days and mini-blocks you choose, schedule them often enough that you will get into a rhythm. As one veteran leader counsels, "Establish a routine of time and place. Unless study is made a regular, habitual part of my schedule, it will constantly be postponed for lack of time."[10]

Let me close this chapter by playing prophet.

If you make block days and mini-blocks part of your life, I predict the following things will happen for you: your thinking will be deeper, your interruptions will be fewer, and your feeling of information overload lighter.

If you choose not to make block days and mini-blocks part of your life, you will probably end up like most other workers: "the glum faces of the folks gobbling lunch at their desks, the ones morosely leaning against the coffee machine wondering how to get everything done by tonight, the walking workplace wounded, the folks who sit strangely hushed as they ride home, bone-tired, soul deflated, job not done, more of the same on the horizon."[11]

It's your choice.

QUESTIONS TO APPLY

- What could a block day give me that my regular workday doesn't?

- What is my biggest concern about taking a block day? What's my biggest obstacle? How could I overcome it?

- How soon could I try a block day? What would be a good date for this experiment?

QUOTES TO TAKE WITH YOU

" The good news is, you're always connected to the office. The bad news is, you're always connected to the office.

—*Ad in the* Wall Street Journal

" The management of time is the management of self.

—*Jill Briscoe*

" If you have so much business to attend to that you have no time to pray, depend upon it, you have more business on hand than God ever intended you should have.

—*D. L. Moody*

chapter 11

TRY AN INFO-TECHNO SABBATH

Only an ancient practice can solve our modern problem

Read this chapter if:

- ❑ You carry a cell phone, a PDA, or a Blackberry.

- ❑ You feel like you can't ever get away from the swarm of information.

- ❑ You feel rushed.

This short chapter offers one idea: Sometimes we must rest from gathering information just as the ancient Israelites rested from gathering wood on the Sabbath.

We must still our racing minds and rest our information-soaked souls. By doing so, we declare that humans do not live by information alone, but by every word that proceeds from the mouth of God.

When Moses hiked down the holy mountain in the hot Middle Eastern sun, carrying stone tablets in his arms, he brought a clear commandment from God: "Tell the people of

Israel to keep my Sabbath day, for the Sabbath is a sign of the covenant between me and you forever. It helps you to remember that I am the Lord, who makes you holy. . . . Work six days only, but the seventh day must be a day of total rest."[1]

The Sabbath, then, had two purposes: rest and remembrance of God. An info-techno Sabbath, as I dub it, has the same goals: rest for our minds and overstimulated senses and remembrance that life is bigger than the news stories, stock quotes, and sports scores. It's bigger than our selves. There is, in fact, a God. And we are not it.

WHY NOBODY LIKES THE IDEA

You'd think that a commandment to take a break would be wildly popular, but the commandment to keep the Sabbath may be broken more than any other. America is one of the most highly churched countries in the world, but consider the percentage of Americans who say they:

Need more fun: 68 percent
Need a long vacation: 67 percent
Often feel stressed: 66 percent
Feel time is crunched: 60 percent
Want less work, more play: 51 percent
Feel pressured to succeed: 49 percent
Feel overwhelmed: 48 percent[2]

Why do we so resist the Sabbath, the simple concept of regular rest? Why fight a chance to unplug from constant information and, as columnist William Safire puts it, "unrestrained reachability"?

The answers to these questions probe into the hot molten core of our motivations. No one has said that better than cultural commentator Ken Myers: "We say we are frustrated by having so much to respond to, but we still carry cell-phones everywhere and check our e-mail every 10 minutes. It makes us feel important to be so busy. Media fasts should help us become more honest about our motivations."[3]

The humble, ancient practice of a Sabbath is really a radical revolution, a coup d'état that overthrows the reigning powers in our life. Information must be not only managed but also dethroned.

"Can't I even bring my laptop?"

(Source: © 2002 Rex F. May, P.O. Box 106, Bellevue, CO 80512. rmay@mac.com. Cartoon #63261. Used with permission)

UNPLUGGING THE GOD OF TECHNOLOGY

To dethrone information, I must dethrone its companion god, technology. On an info-techno Sabbath, I turn off my cell phone, leave my PDA in the drawer, and don't go near the computer, TV, or DVD player. (If you're uncomfortable just reading that, consider your twinge a diagnosis.)

Unplugging from technology does not come easy for me, for I love tech toys. This sounds better than "I have tech lust." I stand in Best Buy before the display case filled with PDAs, staring dreamily at the Compaq ipaq with its sleek stylized case and radiant screen. No worshiper ever stood so reverently before a shrine. I nearly start drooling on the case.

The computer gods keep evolving to a higher level of deity; "since the late 50s, computers have seen 'a 100 thousandfold rise in power' and 'a thousandfold drop in cost.'"[4] I marvel and wonder at their power. Neil Postman explains that technology has become our god "in the sense that people believe technology works, that they rely on it, that it makes promises, that they are bereft when denied access to it, that they are delighted when they are in its presence, that for most people it works in mysterious ways, that they condemn people who speak against it, that they stand in awe of it, and that, in the born-again mode, they will alter their lifestyles, their schedules, their habits, and their relationships to accommodate it."[5]

If an info-techno Sabbath helps us remember the true, living God, then it also pulls us from worship of the deceptive god of technology.

FIVE GIFTS

So consider well the high price of an info-techno Sabbath. But if we are willing to unplug our tech toys, to live for twenty-four hours bereft of incoming information, an info-techno Sabbath also bestows five stunning gifts.

1. Pause. How valuable is a pause from the rapid pace of our lives?

John Ortberg writes: "A Tacoma, Washington, newspaper carried the story of Tattoo the basset hound. Tattoo didn't intend to go for an evening run, but when his owner shut the dog's leash in the car door and took off for a drive with Tattoo still outside the vehicle, he had no choice.

"Motorcycle officer Terry Filbert noticed a passing vehicle with something dragging behind it: it was 'the basset hound picking [up his feet] and putting them down as fast as he could.' The officer chased the car to a stop. Tattoo was rescued, but not before the dog had reached a speed of twenty to twenty-five miles per hour, rolling over several times."

Ortberg concludes, "Too many of us end up living like Tattoo, our days marked by picking them up and putting them down as fast as we can."[6]

If the info-techno Sabbath gave us no other benefit, the gift of pause would be enough. My brain was not designed to run constantly at high RPMs. I need to be freed from speed. I need an info-techno Sabbath to slow down, to remember that haste is not a status symbol. The fact that I'm busier than others does not make me more important.[7]

2. *Perspective.* Unless we observe an info-techno Sabbath, we lose perspective.

Let me say that again: unless we choose to unplug from information for a time, we can never understand that information.

Richard Saul Wurman warns: "Every day the media delivers us more news at a faster rate. We are besieged with accounts of the world in amounts that are impossible to process. As we scramble to keep up with the news race, we are more likely to make errors of perception.... Not only are we more likely to make errors of perception, but the more time we spend with reports of disparate events, the less time we have to understand the factors behind them, to see relationships between them, and to understand the present in the context of history. Instead, we are lulled by a stream of surface facts; we are made numb, passive, and unreceptive by a surfeit of data that we lack the time and the resources to turn into valuable information."[8]

Only by pulling away from information can we hope to gain perspective on it. Only in quiet can we order knowledge. Ordered knowledge is the crown jewel, the rare, sparkling treasure resting on red velvet. A scholar from George Mason University argues that today "the comparative advantage shifts from those with information glut to those with ordered knowledge, from those who can process vast amounts of throughput to those who can explain what is worth knowing, and why."[9]

Speaking for myself, I don't know any way to discern "what is worth knowing" other than an info-techno Sabbath.

Jim, a comptroller and manager in a human-services agency, just began his new job. "I feel overloaded," he admits. "I'm learning an organizational culture that is unfamiliar to me, plus new responsibilities."

"How do you handle that?" I asked.

"Each day I attempt to take time to get in touch with God, one on one. The baseline is prayer. I also make an effort to read a daily devotional online or a small part of the Bible. These things help me put life's information in perspective with eternal information. Through prayer, the Lord helps me change the way I'm thinking about an overloaded situation. In general, I'm reminded that God is in charge, not me."

3. *People.* Something about technology tends to isolate us. But on an info-techno Sabbath, we trade the screen world for the real world. We pull away from gazing at our screens and reconnect with the people in our life.

My wife and I are friends with a couple, Bruce and Nancy, who used to hold "family weekends" once or twice a year. It was like an extended info-techno Sabbath for the family. On those weekends, they explained, nobody answered the telephone. No one did his or her own activities. Instead, the weekend was devoted to spending time with each other.

My wife, Karen, and I liked the idea but weren't sure it could work for us. We had two teenagers. *Will they really want to spend a weekend with their* parents?

Still, we decided to experiment, to try one such weekend, and if it didn't work, we wouldn't do another. We chose a weekend far in advance and kept it open. When that Friday evening finally came, we turned off the phones. No one played games on the computer. No one watched TV alone.

To our surprise, Andrew and Anne loved it. They said the weekend was like a holiday or a vacation. We played games together, watched movies together, and ate together without anyone rushing off.

Scholar Richard Winter says, "It's in the context of relationships that we make the most significant movement and growth in life," but technology undermines those relationships. "Entertainment . . . undermines community in the family because each person sits in front of their own screen. . . . Technology cuts us off from relationships and from reality. Television suggests that life is high drama, love, and sex. Activities such as housework, fundraising, and teaching children to read are vastly underreported. Most pleasures are small pleasures—a hot shower, a sunset, a bowl of good soup, or a good book."[10] On an info-techno Sabbath, we remind ourselves how good the simple pleasures are when shared with people we care about.

4. *Peace.* When I took an editorial job in 1981, there was no email, no fax machine, no pager, no videos, no DVDs, no cell

phone, no Internet, no wi-fi connections. Today we're constantly accessible, and the cell phone that promised to be a link has become a leash. We're interrupted all the time, and so we feel frantic. As one doctor said in exasperation, "I am dying of easy accessibility. If Alexander Graham Bell walked into my office, I'd punch him in the nose. If he called, you can be sure I'd put him on hold."[11]

Now almost every Sunday, I turn off my cell phone and don't check my email. Taking just these two simple steps makes the day more restful and helps clear my mind.

On an info-techno Sabbath, I make myself inaccessible so I can better enter the presence of God. I really must lose my insecurity about knowing everything, my anxiety about not being able to keep up. In God's presence, I regain the peaceful spirit that is of such value in his sight.

5. *Prayer.* When I observe an info-techno Sabbath, I don't read much. If I do read, I limit myself to something that nourishes the soul, and I read slowly, meditatively, with enjoyment.

As good as reading is, it does not rank as the highest form of learning. Martin Luther commented, "I have often learned more in one prayer than I have been able to glean from much reading and reflection."[12] So I take the time I would spend online or answering phone calls, and I reinvest some of it in prayer. One of my favorite writers, François Fénelon, counsels, "You will find some help in the books you have read. What you have read is true and will help you lay a good foundation for your faith. Just do not put too much trust in books, and learn to put them aside as God directs.... God will teach you more than any book or person can. Do you need to go to school to learn how to love God and deny yourself? You already know much more about good than you currently practice. What you need is to put into practice what you already know. Don't try to gain more knowledge before you practice what you already see."[13]

How much do you need a pause in your life? Do you need to gain perspective? Reconnect with people? Regain peace? Enter prayer?

In our age of information, our age of technology, you can receive those wonderful gifts—but you probably won't unless you take the risk and observe an info-techno Sabbath.

QUESTIONS TO APPLY

- Have I ever unplugged from information and technology? If so, what was that experience like? If not, is there something holding me back from doing so?

- What day in the next few months could I try an info-techno Sabbath? What arrangements would I need to make, and whom would I need to notify?

QUOTES TO TAKE WITH YOU

> What is the purpose of a human existence that has become a complex, inescapable stream of data, an overwhelming supply of incitements coming at us from all directions, flashing and beeping and insisting on response, an unprecedented stimulation of the human being?
>
> —*Melinda Davis*[14]

> You do not have to sit outside in the dark. If, however, you want to look at the stars, you will find that darkness is necessary. But the stars neither require nor demand it.
>
> —*Annie Dillard*[15]

chapter 12

WHY WE SECRETLY LIKE OVERLOAD

And how to rework the reasons we don't want to change

Read this chapter if:

- ❏ You have often thought, *I need a less overloaded life*, but haven't made many changes.

- ❏ You sometimes feel hooked on information and the rapid pace of it all.

- ❏ You're ready to take an honest look at yourself so you can change.

As I began writing this book, I set up a breakfast with Alan, an established author. Alan has written more than ten books, speaks regularly at conferences, and teaches every week, so he faces the challenge of information overload. I asked him, "When you hear the phrase 'surviving information overload,' what comes to mind?"

Alan said, "I think, *Can you get addicted to information?* It seems like it."

Hmmm. I hadn't thought about information as something you could get hooked on. I filed Alan's comment but wasn't sure what to make of it.

About that time, my wife, Karen, mentioned my book-in-process to a friend. This woman, a capable administrator at a social services agency, asked, "I wonder if I'm addicted to information." Again, unprompted, the word *addicted*.

Then I read in *Newsweek* David Brooks's satiric description of Wireless Man, who climbs a Rocky Mountain peak but can't enjoy the beauty: "He turns off his phone so he can enjoy a little spiritual bliss. But first, there's his laptop. Maybe somebody sent him an important e-mail. He wrestles with his conscience. His conscience loses. It's so easy to check, after all. . . .

"He sits amid nature's grandeur and says, 'It's beautiful. But it's not moving. I wonder if I got any new voice mails.' He's addicted to the perpetual flux of the information networks. He craves his next data fix. He's a speed freak, an info junkie. He wants to slow down, but can't."[1]

I grinned at this picture of Wireless Man—then felt fear. Since I have a cell phone, a PDA, and a laptop, I, uh, just might resemble Wireless Man.

Might there be something about information—the speed with which it comes, the sense of control it gives us—that can truly become addicting? We find ourselves wanting more information, faster, even when it diminishes our life. Listen to William Van Winkle's confession: "I can live without the Web for a week, but I start getting antsy after a single day without checking my e-mail. At night, I read constantly from the dozen or so periodicals to which I subscribe, while my wife channel-surfs. This is our relaxation time? . . . I feel tired constantly, despite regular exercise, yet continue thinking about the day's information load all the way to unconsciousness.[2]

DESPERATELY SEEKING SOOTHING

Why can information be addictive?

Because, like any addictive substance, information can make us feel good. Let me count the ways.

1. **Control.** Information can give us a sense of control. Right now I'm worrying because my daughter, Anne, has puzzling medical symptoms. First, a blood screen showed abnormally high antibody counts. Then Anne began feeling tingling sensations in parts of her body—knee, arm, hand—at different times. Karen and I immediately set up an appointment with a rheumatologist, as instructed, but it takes three months to get in to see this specialist. In the meantime, I feel anxious. *What is going on? Is it serious or routine?* How much better I will feel when Anne's symptoms have been given a diagnosis. When I hold that information, I will feel calmer and more in control.

2. **Influence.** Information helps you influence others. My friend Rich comments that he thinks "email is particularly addictive because of the sense of affirmation that you get . . . to see that your words can provoke responses, in discussion groups, especially."

3. **Learning.** Learning can be its own reward. The StrengthsFinder inventory (http://www.Strengths Finder.com) reveals your five "signature themes," those innate talents you demonstrate spontaneously and find satisfaction in. One of my signature themes is "Learner: You love to learn. . . . you will always be drawn to the process of learning. The process, more than the content or the result, is especially exciting for you. . . . The thrill of the first few facts, the early

efforts to recite or practice what you have learned, the growing confidence of a skill mastered—this is the process that entices you."[3]

4. **Money.** The careers that pay best generally are those in which you hold information that other people dearly need but can't readily get without you: medicine, computer programming, law, options trading. The Pew Internet and American Life Project Survey found that 52 percent of the heaviest emailers—the information horses—live in households earning at least $75,000 per year, and 32 percent of heavy emailers live in households earning at least $100,000.[4]

5. **Power.** In a work meeting, the person with the best information usually carries the decision. The right information can make the presentation compelling or the article persuasive. Not long ago people in my company disagreed over a major technical question. Whose idea carried? The folks who prepared charts on current usage, estimates on costs, and information on timing.

6. **Speed.** To show that a film character is important, the director shoots him or her walking rapidly into work, past rows of desks and cubicles, back to the corner office. All the way, assistants holding file folders are almost running to keep up and are breathlessly telling the Important Person (editor or senator or detective or boss) about meetings and appointments and decisions; Important Person is firing back what to do, so quickly you can hardly make out the words: "Tell Jones I'll meet him tomorrow cancel the flight to Tokyo and book me to Miami sell the stock I don't care what the constituents say dinner tomorrow at 7 they'll just have

to wait make sure the mayor knows." Speed = importance. Speed = excitement. Speed = adrenaline rush.

When information comes quickly—instant messages on
our PC screen, stock updates on our cell phone—we get
immediate reinforcement and a sense that what we're doing
is important. What we're doing is exciting; it can't wait.

Given these powerful benefits that information confers,
it's not surprising that we start to look forward to getting the
mail, reading the book, or checking the email. Our hearts ask
the information to tell us, "It's okay, it will be all right, you
matter, and you're still in control of life."

Lest you think I'm overstating the pull that information
can have, let me share part of an email I received from a gifted
woman who read an article containing early portions of this
book. She explained: "I'm an orphan, and I don't have any
blood relatives, except for my two children. As a result, I have
spent years searching for all the right answers to life, to ensure
I don't fall short in fulfilling my purpose. I am constantly reading materials to learn as much as I possibly can so I won't be
a failure. Besides all of my inspirational materials (KJV Bible,
NKJV Bible, NIV Bible, Amplified Bible, the Living Bible,
Strong's Concordance and a host of other Bible guides I regularly turn to), I read everything I can get my hands on,
including business periodicals (*The Wall Street Journal, Fortune, Forbes*), books on business leaders (Bill Gates, Jack
Welch, Peter Drucker), and everything I can find on business
management, accounting, real estate, finance, investments. I
even collect annual reports.

"I've been tired in times past and recovered after resting
from information-gathering, but this time is different. This

time, the fatigue I have felt has been lingering for a long time, and I have not been able to find relief. . . . I know that my mental fatigue is my body saying, 'Something is not right.'"[5]

She desperately wanted not to fall short, and information helped her to feel okay, to feel fulfilled. But this very information also began to destroy her. Like most addictive substances, information helps us but can then become overwhelming.

Fortunately, there is a path out of the dark maze of addiction. I must honestly state, though, that the path will require you to crawl through some tight places.

ADMIT WHY WE WANT SO MUCH INFORMATION

First you need to ask some probing questions: *Why do I want so much information? Is it my fear of looking dumb? Is it because I want to get ahead, to make money? I complain about being overloaded, but is there something in the frantic pace that makes me feel important and connected? What's the real reason for squeezing more information into my days and weeks?*[6]

When I was in seventh grade, I brought home an impressive report card: all A's, and one B+. I handed the bright orange testament to my dad, swelling inside a little. I waited for the compliment. My dad looked over the report and then handed it back. "You know," he said, "if you worked a little harder, you could bring up that B+ to an A."

My dad meant to motivate me. But a poison dart stuck in my little eleven-year-old heart. *You need to work harder to really have your dad be excited about you. You need to know everything.*

The problem is that I carried that experience into life. It's easy for me to think my boss and coworkers place that same expectation on me. Sometimes I'm still trying to pull out the dart I received when I was eleven. But I'm not always aware that's what I'm doing. Instead, the dart sticks out in odd behaviors, frustrating to me and incomprehensible to the people around me.

Say I'm talking with friends and someone says, "Have you ever heard of (pick the subject)?" and I haven't. Sometimes I choose the normal, healthy reaction—"No. Tell me about it"—but sometimes I nod as if I have heard of it. I act more knowledgeable than I am. It's a lie, but I must get all A's on the knowledge report card.

Or the college alumni magazine comes in the mail, and I read feature articles about people from my class who now hold Ph.D.'s and chair departments at prestigious colleges. Instead of the normal, healthy reaction—*Hey, that's great they've achieved so much*—I feel a twinge of insecurity and jealousy. *Yeah, well I could have done that too if I'd had the time and money.* I devalue the obvious achievements of people. Why? Apparently I fear that if our graduating class is measured on a curve, I'm getting a C.

Recently I mentioned in a sermon that "in *Bowling Alone*, Harvard researcher Robert D. Putnam points out that over the past twenty-five years in America, the frequency of family dinners is down 33 percent, and having friends over is down 45 percent."[7] After the sermon, a young man told me, "I've been wanting to read *Bowling Alone*. That sounds like an interesting book."

I felt awkward because the fact is I had never read the book. I saw this statistic on a website. So I got the book and read major sections of it, so that if I'm ever quizzed again, A's will appear on some invisible report card. Finally, the dart will be removed. I will be loved. To me, information means never having to say I'm dumb.

I've dwelled longer than I probably should have on my pathology, which I've confessed to God and am gradually changing with God's help. But I'm trying to illustrate how our pains can lead us to relate to information in puzzling and counterproductive ways. Are you willing to confess—to yourself, to a friend, to God—the ways you have asked information or knowledge to tell you you're okay?

OPEN OUR LIVES TO OTHERS

Usually, we can't see on our own the subtle, gossamer webs we've spun. We need people who love us to help us see.

One friend told me, "I used to spend hours reading online message boards and writing postings. I loved it when I caused people to respond, when my words made discussion happen.

"Sometimes I would write a posting that synthesized what people had said and offered a solution. If I offered a solid middle ground or sensible approach, it would end the discussion and no one else would post after that. But instead of feeling good that I had brought the discussion to a profitable end, I would feel disappointed: *No one responded to what I wrote.*

"I was spending hours writing in these online discussions, and my wife one day asked me, 'Why do you spend so much time on that?' I finally realized I was doing it because I wanted the affirmation of seeing people respond to my words."

Is there someone in your life who can see your unhealthy patterns with information overload? Is there someone who will ask you, "Do you really have to check your email right now?"

"You overscheduled again."

ACCEPT OUR RESPONSIBILITY TO SET LIMITS

No matter how many honest friends I cultivate, however, the hard truth is that no one else can manage my life. Am I overloaded with information? If I'm waiting for my boss, a friend, or the geniuses at Microsoft to rescue me, I'm going to wait a long time. In *Courageous Leadership*, Bill Hybels tells this story:

> I came close to a total emotional meltdown in the early 1990s. . . . I remember sitting in a restaurant and . . . putting my head down on my spiral notebook in that restaurant and sobbing.
>
> But I asked myself, *Bill, who has a gun to your head? Who's forcing you to bite off more than you can chew? Who's intimidating you into overcommitting? Whose approval and affirmation and applause other*

than God's are you searching for that makes you live this way?...

The elders, to whom I'm accountable, did not cause my pace problem. It wasn't caused by the board or the staff or family or friends. The whole pace issue was a problem of my own making. I had no one else to blame. . . .

For 15 years, I lived overcommitted and out of control, and deep down I kept saying, *Why aren't the elders rescuing me? Why aren't my friends rescuing me? Don't people see I'm dying here?*

But it isn't their job. It's my job.[8]

Author and speaker Fred Smith coined a phrase I like: "I'm a created being and therefore responsible to the Creator for my life." Since my life is influenced by what I think, I have a responsibility to control information. I must accept the discipline of saying no to constantly answering email, the discipline of unsubscribing to certain publications, and the discipline of admitting that there are many things I don't know and don't have the time to find out.

During the second Gulf War, National Public Radio's "Talk of the Nation" addressed how people coped with the constant news coverage of the war. Most people initially found themselves riveted to the information sources that were on 24-7, but they eventually reached a saturation point. One college student was returning his satellite TV dish because the news had become a major distraction for him, and he knew of no way to stop the hemorrhage of his time but to get rid of that dish.[9] He had accepted his responsibility to set limits.

BE THE SECOND TO KNOW

Speaker Fred Smith tells about "a lawyer friend who won't leave his office without buying a paper for fear 'someone may ask me if I've read something I haven't.' What a tremendous amount of reading time! How much easier to reply, 'No, I didn't see that. What did it say?' The person can tell you in two or three minutes."[10]

It saves time to *not* be the first to know something.

Change your goal from knowing something before anyone else to knowing what you need to know when you need to know it. Nathan Shedroff writes, "There is a dangerous hubris that develops for knowing things first. I'm sure everyone has heard a friend, relative, colleague use a tone of surprised indignation at discovering something considered important that we didn't yet know. In most cases, they are interested in the details and not the meaning."[11]

When we give up the goal of being the first to know, the addictive lure of information loses much of its power. A former editor of a newsmagazine told me, "I am cursed with that journalistic desire to know the news as it happens. But it's rare that I truly need to know the information that fast. The more I let go of the need to know things *right now*, the more I am able to free myself from tyranny-of-the-urgent newsreading."

We don't have to be the first to know. Remember, it's the second mouse to reach the trap who gets the cheese.

CHOOSE LOVE OVER KNOWLEDGE

Shedroff also points out that there's a "common, though mistaken, idea in society that the more we know, the better off we are, and the better person we can be."[12]

Ask yourself if that idea—and I've believed it—is really true. Why, in a society with a historically unparalleled percentage of college-educated citizens, do we also set records for suicides, divorces, and murders? Author Ben Patterson admits, "I'm gradually being disabused of the notion that all this information matters. The Enlightenment suggested that if we could just get more information, we'd be better people. I don't believe that anymore, which has helped me be less compulsive about my reading. The feeling that we've got to read all these things can be an idol."[13]

In my opinion, Christianity offers the world's healthiest view of information: information is valued but never worshiped. By refusing all idols, Christianity also refuses to genuflect before the temple of knowledge. The Christian outlook says that as good as it is to know, it is even better to love. Love is the ultimate definition of what makes me or anyone else a better person. Seventeenth-century mystic François Fénelon captures this view: "You can only know the truth to the degree that you love."[14]

I have an intense drive to know. Do I have the same intense drive to love, to serve, to sacrifice? If I'll stay up late reading, am I willing to stay up late listening to a friend? At the end of my life, when I'm the guest of honor at the funeral, and people are saying overly nice things about me, do I want them to dwell on how much I knew or on how much I cared?

Oh, but it's not that easy. People all around us are subtly telling us that to keep up, to be somebody, to matter, we must gain ever more information, ever more knowledge. My friend Dave, founder and president of a marketing services firm, admits, "There is a lot of fear about not keeping up."

How can we say no to our fears and to people's disapproval when, frankly, we don't know what we're doing, and not knowing could cause us to lose the sale or not get the job or disadvantage our children? I have found help in the confession of the late Yale professor Henri Nouwen, who admitted in an interview, "I cannot continuously say 'No' to this or 'No' to that, unless there is something 10 times more attractive to choose. Saying 'No' to my lust, my greed, my needs, and the world's powers takes an enormous amount of energy. The only hope is to find something so obviously real and attractive that can devote all my energies to saying 'Yes.'... One such thing I can say 'Yes' to is when I come in touch with the fact that I am loved. Once I have found that in my total brokenness I am still loved, I become free from the compulsion of doing successful things."[15]

Do you know that in your total brokenness you are still loved? The Bible reminds us that "Nothing can separate you from God's love. Death can't, and life can't. The angels can't, and the demons can't. Your fears for today, your worries about tomorrow, and even the powers of hell can't keep God's love away."[16]

Say yes to that love, and you will find it easier to say no to the addictive power of information in your life.

Remember the woman I mentioned earlier in this chapter, who was fatigued from information gathering? She concluded her email by saying she found this to be true: "Now I remember that I don't have to know everything. God knows everything. That is all that matters. I can rest in my quest and know and trust that everything in my life will be all right. I don't have to know everything! What a revelation."[17]

QUESTIONS TO APPLY

- When have I most strongly felt that I can't keep up? What does that time teach me about what I fear and what I long for?

- Do I really believe nothing can separate me from God's love? What leads me to answer the way I do?

- Whom can I talk with about this chapter and my responses to it?

QUOTES TO TAKE WITH YOU

  Anxiety is the great modern plague. But faith can cure it.
—*Smiley Blanton*

  O God, help us to be masters of ourselves that we may be servants of others.
—*Sir Alec Paterson*[18]

chapter 13

BLESSED ARE THEY WHO ADMIT THEIR IGNORANCE...

And six other upside-down assumptions to live by

Read this chapter if:

❑ You worry that you can't successfully implement some of the tips and strategies in earlier chapters.

❑ You want a fresh way of thinking about the information overload in your life.

Whenever I set out to solve the problem of too much information in my life, it seems so obvious: I need to battle. I need to learn new strategies, become more efficient, take control.

Efficient strategies to gain control can be helpful, and earlier chapters have offered many such strategies. But I must now offer a final word, a word that may seem shocking and counterintuitive.

Sometimes the best way to gain control is to let go of our need to control. Sometimes the best way to learn is to not know. Sometimes the best way to make a decision is to be less than certain.

I may sound like a zen master spouting koans, but the war against too much information cannot be won by efficiency alone. To conquer information overload, we must also conquer our attitudes. We must defeat overload not only externally but also internally, not only in Microsoft Outlook but also in our own outlook.

Over the years, I have developed seven life-altering maxims. Every one seems odd, counterintuitive, upside-down. But these seven sayings change how I think about information overload, lower my stress, and refresh my soul. I offer them in the form of beatitudes, short sayings pronouncing blessing, much like ones given by Jesus (see Matt. 5:3–12). I encourage all who are information overloaded to meditate on these beatitudes.

☛ *1. Blessed are they who admit their ignorance, for they have found the starting place of knowledge.*

In the late 1980s, my boss's boss called me into his office. I wondered why. "We've just acquired a new magazine called *Christian History,*" Terry explained. "And we think you would make a good editor for the magazine. What do you think?"

I knew exactly what I thought: *I would love that job. Too bad I'm not qualified. I know almost nothing about church history.* "I don't know if I'm the right person," I said candidly. "I've taken only two courses in church history, and I've never studied at the graduate level. People who write for *Christian History* are professional historians who hold doctorates in their field."

"True," Terry said, "but their job is to provide the answers. Your job is to ask the questions."

Seeing that Terry was making a colossal mistake and might soon change his mind, I quickly said yes to the opportunity.

Two weeks later I sat at a desk, editing a magazine on a subject about which I knew zip. I felt excited, and even more anxious. *Someone will quickly figure out I'm an impostor,* I kept thinking.

Over the next few months, I discovered a surprise. My ignorance, which I feared and wanted to hide, was a great asset. Because I didn't know much about the subject, I could not get lost in arcana. I asked the same questions that the reader of the magazine, the "educated nonspecialist," would. I insisted the scholars write in plain English, because otherwise I couldn't understand what they were writing, and this insistence made the magazine comprehensible for 100,000 readers.

Ignorance can be an asset.

Richard Saul Wurman, the provocative architect who wrote *Information Anxiety,* says one of the most powerful ways to deal with information anxiety is to accept your ignorance. "Being able to admit that you don't know is liberating. Giving yourself permission not to know everything will make you relax, which is the ideal frame of mind to receive new information. . . . When you can admit to ignorance, you will realize that if ignorance isn't exactly bliss, it is an ideal state from which to learn."[1]

You may object, "Yes, but how far can ignorance go?"

Well, few feel the pressure to know as much as medical doctors do. But Dr. Richard A. Swenson, author of *The Overload Syndrome,* writes, "It is okay not to know everything. For fifteen years my daily job was tutoring young doctors. When asked a question whose answer I did not know, it was always best to admit ignorance. Even when patients asked such questions, my standard answer was, 'I'm not sure. Let me ask someone who is smarter than I am.' Patients learned to trust me more, not less." [2]

Is there a place in your life where it would help you to admit "I really don't know"? It's in that very place where you will begin to learn.

This leads to a corollary beatitude.

☛ 2. *Blessed are they who know less than others, for they have more teachers.*

We don't always believe this. We think we need to figure it out on our own.

In 1985, product developers at Matsushita Electric Company were trying to develop a home bread-making machine. According to an article in *Harvard Business Review*, "They were having trouble getting the machine to knead dough correctly. Despite their efforts, the crust of the bread was overcooked while the inside was hardly done at all. Employees exhaustively analyzed the problem. They even compared X-rays of dough kneaded by the machine and dough kneaded by professional bakers. But they were unable to obtain any meaningful data.

"Finally, software developer Ikuko Tanaka proposed a creative solution. The Osaka International Hotel had a reputation for making the best bread in Osaka. Why not use it as a model? Tanaka trained with the hotel's head baker to study his kneading technique. She observed that the baker had a distinctive way of stretching the dough." To imitate that, the engineers added special ribs inside the machine and developed a unique 'twist dough' method. In its first year on the market, Matsushita's bread-making machine set a record for sales of a new kitchen appliance. [3]

If you want to make bread, talk to a baker. Duh.

Do you know how to draw out the knowledge and wisdom of the people around you?

First, select consultants, people who can help you in your key learning areas. John Maxwell writes in *Thinking for a Change*: "The people in your life impact your thinking, for better or for worse, so why not work strategically to find people who will stretch you to your potential? Make it a goal to find people who will add value to you in areas that are important to you. . . . This will take your thinking to a whole new level."[4]

Take your short list of key learning areas, the one you drafted in chapter 2. Then write next to each area someone you could go to when you need information or have decisions to make.

My "board of consultants" helps immensely. I call Dave when I have questions about marketing and Brian when I

MY KEY INFORMATION AREAS	CONSULTANTS FOR THIS AREA

have questions about preaching. If I want to know about congregational systems, Lyle gets the call. On midlife issues and spiritual direction, it's Marilyn and Doug. My list could go on. I still need a good consultant on e-commerce, and I'm working to find one. The point is to intentionally select key people who can teach you in your current areas of learning.

(P.S. Your consultants don't have to be older than you. Douglas Rushkoff even argues in *Playing the Future* that today's digital kids—he calls them "screenagers"—are leaders in adapting to today's media-intensive world, and we must learn adaptive skills from them. As one midlife guy told me, "I like to stay in touch with teens or people in college, because there is a freshness about them and an interest in life and learning.")

Then, ask your consultants good questions. This saves time. If I'm writing a book or creating a prototype or thinking about staff issues, I don't try to solve the problems myself. Instead, I generate a rough draft and show it to others. They quickly point out what I'm missing and help me improve my work. As Dr. James Galvin says, "Feedback is the breakfast of champions."

When I wrote chapter 6, "How to Handle Email," I read many websites and articles on the subject. But I gained the most helpful information from Rich Tatum, who works in my company. I asked Rich questions about spam filters, about organizing tools, about list-management software. I admitted my ignorance, and he graciously answered my questions. The result was a better-informed chapter.

Finally, I pay my consultants. Usually, their payment is not in dollars but in the satisfaction of knowing they've made a difference. So I tell them how their counsel has helped me learn or change or grow.

After I finished writing the chapter on email, I sent an email to Rich, saying, "Thank you for your help with the chapter on email. You gave me many vibrant ideas." I wanted him to know that I value his knowledge and time.

☛ *3. Blessed are they who decrease their choices, for they shall increase their time.*

One reason we feel overloaded by information is that we are overloaded by choices. In 1978, there were 11,767 items in the average supermarket; today there are 24,341. Our choices have more than doubled, so we need more information to decide among them.[5] In a brilliant essay in *Harper's*, Thomas de Zengotita, writes, "Compare, say, the cereal and juice sections of a supermarket today with those of years ago. For you youngsters out there, take it from Dad: it used to be Wheaties, Corn Flakes, Cheerios (oats), Rice Krispies—and that was about it. One for each grain, see? Same for fruit juice. But now? Pineapple/Banana/Grape or Strawberry/Orange/Kiwi anyone? And that's just a sample from Tropicana—check out Nantucket Nectars. Makes of cars? Types of sunglasses? Sneaker species? Pasta possibilities? On and on. It's all about options, as they say."[6]

There's only one solution: intentionally decrease your number of choices.

That means you must find a brand you like—even if you don't know about all the other brands and couldn't check them out even if you did—and stick with that brand for now. Choose Tropicana, say, and skip the eight other juice makers. When it comes to information, you don't have time to click through seven satellite channels providing news. Choose (for example) CNN and stick with it.

Melinda Davis, founder and CEO of the Next Group, explains, "As life becomes even more complicated, the consumer will choose a chooser to make choices on her behalf.... Consumers yearn for fewer choices, not more choices, and they will yield to a trusted advocate who will clear a path through the chaos for them."[7] Look for an information source that will give you perspective, that will serve as the fulcrum to help you move the mass of information. Choose only one newspaper, only one or two magazines, and forget the rest.

It's true that whenever you choose one information source, you give up something. You give up the additional perspective you might get from a different source. But today, when there are hundreds of satellite radio stations and tens of thousands of Internet radio stations, you have to choose. By decreasing your choices, you increase your time. As George Trow reminds us, "The aim is to have chosen successfully, not to be endlessly choosing."[8]

☛ *4. Blessed are they who are less than certain, for they shall certainly make better decisions.*

I know three highly educated women who are new moms, and all of them, in the words of one, "research a parenting topic from every different angle before I can feel comfortable with a decision. Every major decision with a newborn baby has so many different opinions (Cloth or disposable? Share a bed or separate crib? Breast or bottle? Nurse to sleep or let baby learn to sleep on his own?). I find myself overwhelmed with the options for every single decision."

The challenge for new mothers and for all of us is to know, "When do I have enough information to make this decision? When do I know enough to feel comfortable?"

It used to be that to make a good decision, you got all the information you could. Not now. Today, when there's too much information available, you must do something counterintuitive: limit the amount of information you study before you make your decision. You can no longer indulge in the luxury of studying every word on the issue and reaching 100 percent certainty on the decision. Instead, you must learn to live with less than absolute confidence that you're making the right decision.

My practice is this: I try to get enough information so that I feel 85 percent certain I'm making the right decision. When I reach the 85 percent certainty level, I don't have every question answered. I know there are risks. But I feel heavily weighted toward one option. When I feel 85 percent certain, I don't keep gathering information; I just make the call.

Doesn't this mean I sometimes make the wrong decision? Yes. Shouldn't I spend the time to get enough information so that I am 100 percent confident my decision is right? No. It's usually impossible, given the acres of information available, to go over every inch of ground. But even if I could gain enough information to reach 100 percent certainty, spending that much extra time and energy rarely proves worth it.

Sometimes, though, I can't reach even 85 percent certainty. Too many variables remain unknown and unknowable. For example, last year our company had to decide whether to buy a content-management software package or develop it ourselves. I sat in a group discussing the options, and we all felt the high stakes: hundreds of thousands of dollars and months of staff time. But since this area of software development is still new, there wasn't enough history to determine whether it's better to build or to buy. We couldn't find all the information we wanted, especially for a decision of this magnitude. What to do?

In a case like this, when I can't reach 85 percent certainty, I'm willing to live with 65 percent certainty. I go ahead and make the decision.

If you and your team have reached a certainty level of 85 percent, or failing that, 65 percent, then stop searching for information. Don't hide your fear behind "We're continuing to gather information." Make the decision. Pull the trigger. Better to make a decision than to stand frozen, for if you make a decision and it proves to be wrong, you'll soon know it and can adjust accordingly.

Yes, it's paradoxical, but in our age of information overload, it's nonetheless true: Blessed are they who are less than certain, for they shall certainly make better decisions.

☛ 5. *Blessed are they who are stimulus-poor, for they shall be experience-rich.*

If you ever decide you want to become bored and cynical, I can tell you how to do it. My solution is easy; anyone can do it, and it doesn't cost much.

Simply watch a lot of TV and a lot of movies.

In his book *Still Bored in a Culture of Entertainment*, Richard Winter explains that "overstimulation can lead to boredom as much as understimulation."[9] And in *Media Unlimited: How the Torrent of Images and Sounds Overwhelms Our Lives*, Todd Gitlin argues that today's heavy stimulus of electronic impulses leads to fatigue, numbness, and cynicism.[10]

Is this just the clucking of bookworm academics? I'm sorry to say, no. Today, when the average teenager watches more than 100 movies per year, we have to ask, "What is our high consumption of movies and TV doing to us?"[11] The answer, according to an increasing number of researchers, is one or more of the following: (1) we gradually lose the capacity to think deeply and creatively; (2) we become bored; (3) our faith is eroded; (4) we find it more difficult to delay gratification; (5) we damage the quality of our relationships.[12]

I won't go on, for no one wants to talk about this. We're not addicted to visual stimulation, we aver, but if you take away our TV and movies, we get jittery and angry. One year, on a sort of spiritual dare, my friend Eric gave up TV for six weeks. Before he started, he confessed his anxieties: "I would miss March Madness. I'd have no water cooler patter to share with the Must-see crowd. *Voyager* might reach home without me. Everybody loves Raymond—except me."[13]

Despite his anxiety, Eric kept the TV off for those six weeks. Here's what happened to him and his wife: "We go to sleep a little earlier, we read more carefully, we talk more deeply—when we choose to talk. And we listen." Not so bad. In fact, the couple liked what happened so much, they now forgo TV every March.

Much of the reason we feel overloaded by information is that we feel overstimulated—too many DVDs in too little time. And we sense but can't say, "There is an inverse correlation between the amount of TV and movies I watch and the richness of my experience." One friend lamented, "I don't know why, but my wife and I will stay up late watching people on TV have sex, but we won't turn off the set, go to our bedroom, and enjoy sex ourselves."

Professor Barbara Brown Taylor finally made a decision: "I've intentionally narrowed my time with media. . . . I'm more interested in immediate experience. A lot of media is just what it sounds like: mediated experience, vicarious experience. The more time I spend consuming it or feeling as if I have to consume it all, I miss my life, miss what God is doing right in front of me. So I'm more interested now in who I run into at the grocery store or what I see a kid doing at the park or what story I hear from the person who needs emergency assistance or what I hear in the hospital. At this point in my life, that's how I want to learn about the world."[14]

Would you like your life to be rich with experience—direct experience, your own experience? Would you like to deepen friendships and heighten meaning? You can have that life, but it comes at a price, a price few are willing to pay. You have to intentionally narrow your time with media.

🐾 6. *Blessed are they who make small changes, for they shall see big results.*

If you've read this far, you must be motivated. You're probably ready to make big changes in your life. This beatitude recommends just the opposite: Make small changes.

Adjust your information practices, even slightly, and over time you'll find increasing peace and productivity. Make small changes, and you will see big results.

Unsubscribe to one email newsletter. Throw out a newsmagazine without looking at it. Turn off the TV half an hour earlier at night. These may be small, bonsai-size changes, but if kept to, they will reduce the information in your life and give you more space to think and rest and apply.

Author Dave Goetz draws an analogy from fly-fishing in Colorado mountain streams. "In the sport of fly-fishing, the primary goal is to cast into the stream or river an imitation of a bug so it appears to be real—a real mosquito or ant or grasshopper or mayfly.... The fly-fisher's goal is to cast upstream and then let the fly float downstream in a 'dead-drift,' in which the imitation insect flows along with the current as naturally as possible. This is painfully difficult to execute.

"To create a dead-drift, the fly-fisher mends the fly-line as the fly floats downstream . . . flipping only the line that lies on the surface. . . . The better one is at mending, the better the results. . . .

"The trick for the lover of God is to learn how to become better at mending one's life, to make small adjustments on a regular basis to avoid the speed and clutter of modern living."[15]

Mend your line. Make a small change. One small change, followed up on, will make more difference in your life than one big change that is implemented and then forgotten.

☛ 7. *Blessed are they who expect less from information, for they shall receive more from life.*

Information cannot necessarily lead us to the great ideas of life.

Think about the Constitution's main concept, "All men are created equal," on which American society is founded. Theodore Roszak writes, "Those who shed their blood over the generations to defend that assertion (or to oppose it) did not do so on the basis of any data presented to them. The idea has no relationship whatever to information. One would be hard pressed even to imagine a line of research that might prove or disprove it."[16]

Thus, we shouldn't expect information alone to get us where we most need to go. Often in life we may need to move to the point where facts thin and then vanish. "For there," Roszak adds, "we find what might be called the *master ideas*— the great moral, religious, and metaphysical teachings which are the foundations of culture."[17]

This frees us from the tyranny of desperately seeking information. We can accept information's value without expecting too much. Says my friend Lee: "I've learned that lots of information is a poor substitute for simply thinking. Insight matters more than information. Wisdom has always been in short supply, and wisdom builds from very basic principles, not generally from mountains of information."

Give up the notion that if you knew more, your life would be much better. Nathan Shedroff writes that there's a "common, though mistaken, idea in society that the more we know, the better off we are, and the better person we can be."[18]

Really?

Listen to these probing questions from Neil Postman:

> If children die of starvation in Ethiopia, does it occur because of a lack of information? Does racism in South Africa exist because of a lack of information? If criminals roam the streets of New York City, do they do so because of a lack of information?
>
> Or, let us come down to a more personal level: If you and your spouse are unhappy together, and end your marriage in divorce, will it happen because of a lack of information? If your children misbehave and bring shame to your family, does it happen because of a lack of information? If someone in your family has a mental breakdown, will it happen because of a lack of information?
>
> I believe you will have to concede that what ails us, what causes us the most misery and pain—at both cultural and personal levels—has nothing to do with the sort of information made accessible by

computers. The computer and its information cannot answer any of the fundamental questions we need to address to make our lives more meaningful and humane. The computer cannot provide an organizing moral framework. It cannot tell us what questions are worth asking. It cannot provide a means of understanding why we are here or why we fight each other or why decency eludes us so often, especially when we need it the most.[19]

Blessed are we when we know that it takes more than information to create a meaningful life.

QUESTIONS TO APPLY

- Which of these beatitudes hit me most? Why?

- How could I remember and reflect on that beatitude?

QUOTES TO TAKE WITH YOU

" The principles closest to my heart—and the most radical—are learning to accept your ignorance, paying more attention to the question than the answer, and never being afraid to go in an opposite direction to find a solution.

—*Richard Saul Wurman*[20]

" Information is overrated, and curiosity is underrated.

—*Lee Eclov*[21]

part 4

BONUS
Stuff

Hey, it doesn't cost you anything extra

chapter 14

GREAT INFORMATION ON INFORMATION

A short guide to resources that are helpful—
and some that aren't

Read this chapter if:

❑ You want to keep learning about how to survive information overload.

❑ You are curious which authors and resources helped shape this book.

Maybe you'd like to learn more about surviving information overload. Or maybe you just want to know where I got some of my ideas. Either way, here's a list.

To model the virtue of providing only the information people need, I kept the list short. (Okay, it probably could have been shorter.) I also added brief comments, so you could see what's helpful (or not) about each resource. Finally, I gave each item a "Miller Rating," ranging from 1 M (low) to 5 Ms (high). That way, you can make informed choices about the resources that will help you.

ⓘ WEB GENERAL SEARCH

The web is not a good place to study information overload. Let me explain why.

When I began doing research for this book, I went to http://www.google.com and typed in *"information overload."* I expected a few thousand results. I got 587,000. Am I the only one who sees a bitter irony here? It would take me four years to click on 587,000 links, let alone read them all.

Worse, that number is rapidly growing. Half a year later, when I wanted to verify the number of 587,000 before putting it in print, I searched Google again. This time, search-engine results had jumped to 725,000, giving me another 138,000 results to wade through.

You can narrow results, though, by using the one search engine that understands that less is more: Mamma.com. Search on *"information overload"* and Mamma serves up only 65 results, with eight of the first ten highly relevant. ***Miller Ratings:*** Google, M. Mamma, MMM.

ⓘ WEB DIRECTORY SEARCH

Some search engines offer a topical directory, which can help immensely, because editors (usually volunteers) assign websites to specific topics. In the Google directory (http://www.google.com/dirhp), follow this path: Reference → Knowledge Management → Information Overload. Then choose from one of eight topics: Effects, Email Overload, Hypertext, Knowledge Discovery, Personal Organization, Relevance Filtering, Speed Reading, or Time Management. The greatest practical guidance falls under three of those: Email Overload, Personal Organization, and Time Management.

Still, expect some undesirable results, such as the highly technical (for example, "Explores a hybrid learning algorithm applied to the problem of Information Intake Filtering—IIF") or organizational (such as the official website of the Email Management Benchmarking Association, the EMMBA. Bet their conventions are a blast.).

Alta Vista also offers a topical directory, but following it through either Reference or Education, you hit dead ends for the subject of information overload. And the sponsored matches, annoyingly, look like regular matches.

Miller Ratings: Google directory, MM. Alta Vista directory, zero Ms.

① SPECIFIC WEBSITES AND WEB PAGES

I hope I'm not being unnecessarily rigorous in my evaluation, but I haven't found many websites that help with information overload. A few exceptions:

- "Fact Sheet 4: Reducing Junk Mail" by the Privacy Rights Clearinghouse offers clear, practical help for reducing paper junk mail (http://www.privacy rights.org/fs/fs4-junk.htm). *Miller Rating:* MMMM.
- OvercomeEmailOverload.com mostly promotes books but freely offers "top ten tips" on handling email, by Kaitlin Duck Sherwood. *Miller Rating:* MMM.
- In the left-hand column of SearchEngineWatch.com, click on Web Searching Tips. The helpful articles you will find include "Search Engine Math" and "Power Searching for Anyone," by Danny Sullivan, though the

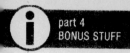
information is somewhat outdated. *Miller Rating:* MMM.

- "Information Overload: Fighting Data Asphyxiation Is Difficult but Possible," by William Van Winkle, in the archives of ComputerBits: http://www.computer bits.com/archive/1998/0200/infoload.html. *Miller Rating:* MMM.

- Browsing the "Information/Work Overload Annotated Webliography" (http://www.softpanorama.org/Social/ overload.shtml) is like shopping at a thrift store: too much to paw through, but sometimes you find a delightful overlooked item. *Miller Rating:* MMM.

ⓘ BOOKS

- If you read only one book on information overload, read *Information Anxiety* by Richard Saul Wurman (Doubleday, 1989). Wurman is the architect, genius, curmudgeon, and designer who developed the Access guidebooks, and this is his landmark work on "the ever-widening gap between what we understand and what we think we should understand." Wurman points out that we have too much data and not enough knowledge but then shows how to bridge that gap. Plus, the book is simple to scan and beautifully designed. *Miller Rating:* MMMMM.

- The sequel, *Information Anxiety 2* (Que, 2001) is likewise clear, hope-producing, and filled with enjoyable examples. *Miller Rating:* MMMM.

- For a Christian perspective, read Dr. Richard Swenson's *Margin: Restoring Emotional, Physical, Financial, and Time Reserves to Overloaded Lives* (NavPress,

1992) or *The Overload Syndrome: Learning to Live within Your Limits* (NavPress, 1998). Drawing on extensive research and his medical background, Swenson convinces you that our culture's desire for "more and more, faster and faster" is toxic. ***Miller Rating:*** MMMM.

- *Breathing Space: Living and Working at a Comfortable Pace in a Sped-Up Society* by Jeffrey P. Davidson (MasterMedia, 1991). I worried when this book, which is "guaranteed to help you handle the deluge of information," started with nine pages of endorsements. But I liked the book's simplicity and practicality. You'll gain ideas you can implement. ***Miller Rating:*** MMMM.

- *Managing Information Overload* by Lynn Lively (AMACOM, 1996). If it's possible for a book to be too simple, this ninety-four-page workbook might be (for example, "Put your name and today's date at the top of three pieces of paper.") Still, if you're overloaded, you may need someone to walk you by the hand, and this book does that. ***Miller Rating:*** MMM.

- Richard Carlson, Ph.D., *Don't Sweat the Small Stuff at Work: Simple Ways to Minimize Stress and Conflict while Bringing Out the Best in Yourself and Others* (Hyperion, 1998). Carlson almost convinces you the solutions to information overload are simple. Then you realize, *If they were this easy, we would all be keeping up and wouldn't need this book.* ***Miller Rating:*** M.

① BOOK CHAPTERS

Business executive Fred Smith comments, "I'm surprised at how many people feel they have to read a book cover to cover. If I'm in a hurry, I skim the table of contents, find the subjects I need to know about immediately, and read those chapters. I'm a firm believer in not eating the whole pie. One piece gives plenty of ideas."[1]

- It seems a shame to apply Fred's advice to his book *Learning to Lead: Bringing Out the Best in Others* (Leadership/Word, 1986), since it's well worth reading in its entirety. But on the subject of overload, read chapter 5, "An Emergency Plan for Saving Time," and chapter 6, "Winning the War for Time." *Miller Rating:* MMMMM.
- Who other than Peter Drucker can remind us that "the current Information Revolution is actually the fourth Information Revolution in human history" and then draw lessons from the first three to help us with this one? Don't miss chapters 4 and 5 in *Management Challenges for the Twenty-first Century* (Harper Business, 1999). *Miller Rating:* MMMM.
- "Enlarging the Mind to Expand the Ministry," chapter 6 of *Mastering Personal Growth* by Maxie Dunnam, Gordon MacDonald, and Donald W. McCullough (Multnomah, 1992), shows what to study and what to ignore. Written for pastors but valuable for all leaders. *Miller Rating:* MMMM.
- "Clearing the Clutter" by John Maxwell, chapter 4 in *The Time Crunch: What to Do When You Can't Do It All* (Christianity Today/Multnomah, 1993), convinced me I needed to trust the people around me more and thereby reduce the load on my own desk. *Miller Rating:* MMMM.
- Okay, this chapter offers no solutions, but it is unexcelled in its pained description of our increasing inabil-

ity to read, write, and think deeply: "Why Bother?" in *How to Be Alone* by Jonathan Franzen (Farrar, Straus and Giroux, 2002). *Miller Rating:* MMM.

- Chapter 9 of *Ordering Your Private World* by Gordon MacDonald (Oliver-Nelson, 1984) is like a coach's strong pep talk on training yourself to think and study. *Miller Rating:* MMM.

ⓘ MAGAZINE ARTICLES AND MONOGRAPHS

- If you don't have time to read *Information Anxiety*, my top book recommendation, here's a good précis: Richard Saul Wurman, "Redesign the Data Dump: As the Author of 1989's *Information Anxiety* Proves Again, 'Information Architecture' Still Has a Long Way to Go," *Business 2.0* (November 28, 2000), pages 210–22. *Miller Rating:* MMMM.

- David Brooks, "Time to Do Everything Except Think," *Newsweek* (April 30, 2001), brilliantly diagnoses the pathologies caused by too much information. *Miller Rating:* MMMM.

- Thomas de Zengotita does the same thing, only with deeper, more poignant description, in *Harper's* magazine (April 2002): "The Numbing of the American Mind: Culture as Anesthetic." *Miller Rating:* MMMMM.

- *Email at Work*, by Deborah Fallows, senior research fellow, The Pew Internet and American Life Project Survey (December 8, 2002). Provides accurate, believable data on how workers use email and how they feel about it. Surprise: they basically like it. *Miller Rating:* MMMM.

- Andy Crouch, columnist for *Christianity Today*, has written three incisive and witty columns on our idolatry of

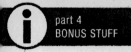

technology: "Promises, Promises" (February 19, 2001); "Grounded" (November 12, 2001); and "Rekindling Old Fires" (August 5, 2002). *Miller Rating:* MMM.

ⓘ AUDIO

- Dan Sullivan, *The Time Breakthrough* (Strategic Coach, 2001). Sullivan, a coach and consultant to entrepreneurs, argues that we all have enough time; he then helps us set priorities. To order, go to http://www.strategiccoach.com or call 1-800-387-3206. *Miller Rating:* MMM.
- *Mars Hill Audio Journal,* volume 59, November/December 2002. Ken Myers interviews Todd Gitlin, author of *Media Unlimited: How the Torrent of Images and Sounds Overwhelms Our Lives* (Metropolitan, 2001), who points out how media distract us from both interior and exterior concerns but also that we want them to. Then Myers talks with Calvin College professor Quentin Schultze, author of *Habits of the High-Tech Heart: Living Virtuously in the Information Age* (Baker, 2002). Schultze says our culture's two highest values are efficiency and control but points out that these are not virtues, and they tend to move us away from virtue. To order, go to http://www.marshillaudio.org. *Miller Rating:* MMM.

ⓘ PEOPLE

To survive information overload, increasingly we must study the "living human documents," as Barbara Brown Taylor writes. People who have helped me most with information overload—through their conversations, lives, and writings—

cluster in several groups, which I've listed alphabetically. Write your own list and see how it compares to mine. Then spend more time with people from those groups.

- **Artists.** They see the whole; they break through data gridlock by flying above it. For me, this list would include architect Richard Saul Wurman *(Information Anxiety)*, sculptor Gordon MacKenzie (*Orbiting the Giant Hairball*), and *Christian History* designer Rai Whitlock.

- **Cross-cultural friends.** People who grew up in Latin America or Africa don't seem to feel the pressure I do about information; they move to a slower pace, one that allows more dancing, joy, and wonder. My friends Iyke Ugo, Rossi Crissien Tretbar, and Nori Menendez-Borelly have helped me here.

- **Leaders.** They cut through clutter with great focus and efficiency, and the finest leaders use those skills to bring out the best in others. Fred Smith (*Learning to Lead* and BreakfastwithFred.com), my boss Paul Robbins, and Max DePree (*Leadership Jazz* and *Leadership Is an Art*) stand as examples for me.

- **Mystics.** Those who experience God profoundly solve the problem of overload by asking the deepest questions of life: Who am I? Who am I becoming? and Whom do I worship? In this class I place Mother Teresa (*My Life for the Poor*, or even better, *Something Beautiful for God* by Malcolm Muggeridge), François Fénelon (*The Seeking Heart* presents his stunning thoughts in modern English), Henri Nouwen (*Life of the Beloved*), Richard Foster (*Celebration of Discipline*), and Thomas Merton *(The Seven-Storey Mountain)*. I

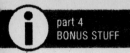

also include my friend Brian Larson *(Running the Midnight Marathon)*.

- **Question askers.** People who ask probing questions stop me, make me think, help me change. I'm grateful to consultant Lyle Schaller *(Discontinuity and Hope; The Interventionist;* and dozens of other books) and entrepreneur Dave Goetz (CustomZines.com) for their willingness to dig for truth, even if that requires a few carefully placed sticks of dynamite.

- **Reference librarians.** These people will go to heroic lengths to answer my questions or find the source I need—and they do it for free.

QUESTIONS TO APPLY

- Which sources have most helped me with information overload? What made them helpful?

- Which one or two sources listed above would be most valuable to me at this point in my life?

QUOTES TO TAKE WITH YOU

" The Library of Congress contains more than 100 million documents housed on 650 miles of shelving.

—*Richard A. Swenson*[2]

" The beautiful, the good, the true cannot be weighed and measured. True knowledge is spiritual knowledge, which is beyond the reach of the world of quantity and therefore is disregarded by our civilization.

—*Paul Tournier*

A WORD FOR CHURCH LEADERS

Facing the unique pressures of information overload for pastors

Read this chapter if:

- ❑ You are a pastor or church leader, or you are married to one.

- ❑ You wonder about the connection between information overload and Christianity.

I've spent my entire adult life serving and providing resources for church leaders, so I hope my other readers will forgive me a brief word for pastors.

As a pastor, you do not necessarily deal with more information than, say, a computer programmer, a comptroller, or a journalist. But the role does present some unique challenges:

† You have to stand up and say something fresh and profound two or more times a week. We would never place this daunting requirement on motivational speakers (who reuse a speech many times), comedians (who perform the same routine), or

television scriptwriters (who play reruns between new episodes). This Olympian demand calls for vigorous training: reading, studying, learning.

(Not to mention that public speaking strikes fear in the hearts of most normal people, causing anxiety and frantic thoughts of *I've got to be prepared*. I recently read that more people feared speaking in public than feared dying. That means that if these people were at a funeral, they'd rather be the person in the casket than the one delivering the eulogy.)

† People want a relationship with their pastor; they hope the pastor will understand their world to some degree. Consequently, pastors may feel, more than most people, pressure to be omni-knowledgeable, to speak intelligently to the concerns of the bond trader, the single mother, the Montessori teacher, the widower in failing health, and the long-haul trucker. To some degree, each parishioner hopes the pastor will connect with his or her world, speak the language, share the concerns.

John Stott even calls this knowledge a pastoral responsibility: "If we are to build bridges into the real world, and seek to relate the Word of God to the major themes of life and the major issues of the day, then we have to take seriously both the biblical text and the contemporary scene. We cannot afford to remain on either side of the cultural divide. . . . It is our responsibility to explore the territories on both sides of the ravine until we become thoroughly familiar with them."[1]

† The pastoral role stretches like a huge canvas tent over many different areas. A university president or business entrepreneur may be the only jobs that approach a pastor's for the variety of subjects that need to be mastered. In the case of a pastor, these subjects include: theology, biblical

studies, counseling, family dynamics, youth ministry, nursery security, organizational liability, crisis intervention, capital fundraising, zoning, architecture, worship styles, small groups, congregational systems, leadership, mentoring, prayer, sexuality, education, preaching, spiritual direction, local politics, community organization, singles issues, alcoholism, volunteer recruitment, and many more.

Combine these challenges, and it's no wonder that my pastor friend Lee says, "I generally feel overloaded. The ministry is, among other things, a knowledge profession. Books and articles are our stock in trade. Plus, I made a commitment to read outside of my professional area—to read novels, history, news. Then, it seems we pastors are always trying to learn some new technology or software."

A MODEST PROPOSAL

In the spirit of wanting to lighten the heavy load you carry, I offer the following suggestions. Select any you find helpful and ignore the rest: enjoy the fish while spitting out the bones.

† Try not to base your expectations on what other pastors do. It makes no sense to compare yourself to anyone. Even if the Bible didn't forbid it, which it does (Gal. 6:4), each person possesses unique and unrepeatable strengths that cannot be duplicated by you or anyone else. Martin Luther may have translated the New Testament into German in an astonishing eleven weeks. I grant that Charles Haddon Spurgeon read six books of dense Puritan theology every week, and carrying only one page of notes into the pulpit, he could preach a forty-minute sermon so penetrating and artful that people still read it today. A minister across town may possess stellar gifts of

teaching, wisdom, and knowledge, and some people may leave your church to attend his or hers, which hurts.

But to quote Jesus, as he said when Peter was unhealthily focusing on his fellow apostle John: "What is that to you?" God has given you the level of knowledge and wisdom you need to serve in the ministry he has called you to. No one can make the impact you can, with your gifts, passions, interests, and opportunities.

† Believe what the theology texts say about God's sovereignty. I love these words by Fred Smith: "Our responsibility, our talent, and our time are all given by God. If he can't balance these, who can? One of the most unstressing things I ever discovered was that God could exist after I died! That was most revealing. Why should I feel all this pressure? After all, what would change between the moment I'm doing all this work and the moment I'm dead? Nothing as far as God is concerned. So I don't have to fret; he didn't intend me to live with all this pressure."[2]

† Balance left-brain reading (commentaries, theology, philosophy, history) with right-brain reading (novels, short stories, poetry).

At least two times I've prayed for pastors who came to me in desperation, saying, "I can't seem to hear from God. Other people get words, Scriptures, visions, and dreams, but it's as if I can see and hear nothing." As I talked with these pastors (both men), I discovered that for years, both had read nothing but commentaries and theological works. No novels, no poems, no fantasy literature, no books on great paintings. Their intuitive, symbolic, and imaginative faculties had atrophied from lack of use, limiting the ways they could hear from God and express those messages.

I strongly prefer nonfiction to fiction, too, so I must intentionally select works that exercise the right side of my brain. Clearly the God who inspired not only the law codes of Leviticus but also the heady visions of Ezekiel would like us to take in both precept and picture.

A Midwestern pastor says, "I heard Warren Wiersbe comment on how he has many books going at once because of his varying moods. That gave me permission to have two or three books (no more) going at once, as long as they are distinctly different—for example, a novel and a book about ministry."

† Rely on recommendations from other people as a filter for your reading. Pastors generally possess people skills in abundance, so why not use those to lighten your information load? Says one pastor I respect, "I rely on others and ask other pastors, 'What have you found helpful?'" Another pastor who uses this approach says, "I've decided to let my staff be the experts in various fields. I let them tell me what I should be reading in their area to stay current. But even then I don't read everything they send me. Only when an article or book or movie is suggested to me more than once by different people on unrelated occasions—that's when I determine that I have to look at it."

The wise Eugene Peterson offers a nice recommended reading list in *Take and Read* (Eerdmans, 1996).

† Feel free to skip over familiar concepts. You're not being graded on whether you read every page in the book. A friend in ministry told me, "Long ago someone suggested the simple idea, 'Don't read what you already know.' So when I'm reading a book and I realize the next paragraph or page is something I know or understand, I skip on till I hit something new or fresh."

† Plan for the distance, not the dash. Billy Graham was speaking to a group of ministers in London, and one asked him, "If you had your ministry to do over again, what would you do differently?"

Graham thought and then said, "I've preached too much and studied too little." His balance of public ministry and private study worked well for the short term, apparently, but not, he now realized, for the long term. How can you build into that balance a pattern of study that will benefit you both now and ten years from now?

"Next Sunday's sermon title? 'The Simplicity of the Gospel.'"

(Source: © 1989 Wendell Simons. Used with permission.)

Some pastors I know take a summer study break, when the pace of ministry is somewhat lighter. One pastor asks selected church members to preach occasionally, so he can get a break. Another formed a regional group of four pastors who preach on the same topics or texts each week, and group members share their ideas and content beforehand. Still another pastor created a reading club, in which church members read books that he wants to read but doesn't have time for. He trains the club members in what to look for, and they flag material for preaching, as well as summarize a book's key concepts.

MY TOP TWELVE WEBSITES FOR PREACHERS

More than any other pastoral duty, preaching brings pressure for learning. "I think I feel special pressure as I begin preaching from a new book or portion of the Bible," says one pastor. "I feel as though I should read up on the background information in commentaries, etc., but I just can't get to it. I'm embarrassed about that deficit."

So I offer here my favorite websites for preachers. As a preacher myself, I need accurate, timely information, and thus, often rely on the web. But maybe you've felt, as I have, that there are too many websites, and many of those are not worth the time. Thus, my short list of sites, which does not include sites that primarily offer full-text sermons. Not that we can't draw on others' material, within guidelines, but this list is for those who will be doing their own writing.

1. For Bibles in various translations (and languages), my favorite site is **Bible Gateway** (http://bible.gospel com.net). You can search easily by word or Bible verse.

2. For general reference and fact checking, I like **RefDesk.com,** which calls itself "the single best source for facts on the Net," and it just might be.

3. If you don't find what you need at RefDesk.com, check **Library Spot,** a portal to virtually any information a library contains.

4. I have not found a full-orbed online source of commentaries. Dozens of sites offer the dated Matthew Henry commentary, and Blue Letter Bible (http://cf.blueletterbible.org/commentaries/) adds Calvin and Spurgeon and Chuck Smith, but the web is begging for contemporary biblical scholarship. The best I've seen so far: many of **InterVarsity Press's New Testament commentaries** (http://www.biblegateway.com/cgi-bin/webcommentary).

5. To stay fresh on the world of ideas, check out **Arts and Letters Daily** (http://www.aldaily.com).

6. For a similar site from a Christian perspective, see **Books and Culture** (http://www.booksandculture.net/).

7. For religious news, **Christianity Today** (http://www.christianitytoday.com/ctmag) provides daily updates and analysis that is fair and accurate.

8. Odd tidbits, often useful for setting up a preaching topic, startle you at **News of the Weird** (http://www.newsoftheweird.com/archive/index.html).

9. For clean humor, *Reader's Digest* includes the famous humor columns from the magazine (http://www.rd.com/; click on In This Issue, and then on Fun).

10. Want summaries of the latest books by evangelical authors, such as Max Lucado and Mark Buchanan?

You'll find those in PDF files at http://www.**Christian BookSummaries.com.**

11. You can find the Christian classics, in one place, from Albertus Magnus to John Woolman, at **Christian Classics Ethereal Library** (http://www.ccel.org).

12. For sermon illustrations, I'm admittedly biased, because I helped create this site, but www.**Preaching Today.com** offers high-quality material I can (and do) actually preach.

LET'S CLOSE IN PRAYER

In parting, let me share this prayer by Richard Kriegbaum in *Leadership Prayers:*

> If I were brilliant, if I had the knowledge and strengths that I admire in so many other people, if I were a spiritual giant, I would simply ask you to help me do my best. But my best is not good enough. I do not know enough, and I cannot see clearly enough. I am your child, and I want to learn, but unless your Spirit teaches me, I have little to offer. I need your wisdom.
>
> What you give me determines the success or failure of those I lead. They deserve some word, they need a message. How else will they understand our situation and how it informs our direction and points to a worthy purpose? I have studied and analyzed all I can. Teach me to go beyond the facts and feelings. My spirit waits quietly. I need your wisdom.
>
> Teach me, God, so I have some wisdom to share.[3]

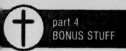

QUESTIONS TO APPLY

- When in my ministry do I most feel information overload or that I can't keep up? How can I convert that feeling into prayer?

- What in this chapter is most helpful to me right now? What should I do as a result?

QUOTES TO TAKE WITH YOU

" Thanks be to God for a life full-packed with things that matter, crying to be done.

—*John Oxenham*

" O Lord, renew our spirits and draw our hearts unto thyself, that our work may not be to us a burden, but a delight.

—*Benjamin Jenks*

The table in chapter 1 by Richard A. Swenson is © 1992 by Richard A Swenson, M.D. Reprinted by permission from *Margin: Restoring Emotional, Physical, Financial, and Time Reserves to Overloaded Lives* (Colorado Spring: NavPress, 1992). All rights reserved. www.navpress.com.

The cartoon in chapter 2 is © 1980 by Rob Portlock. Used with permission. All rights reserved.

The cartoon in chapter 3 is © 1990 by Steve Phelps. Used with permission. All rights reserved.

The cartoon in chapter 4 is © 1983 by *Leadership*. Concept: David MCasland. Art: Frank Baginski. Used with permission.

The cartoon in chapter 10 is © 1986 by *Leadership*. Concept: David L. McAllister. Art: Ron Wheeler. Used with permission.

The cartoon in chapter 11 is © 2002 by Rex F. May. P.O. Box 106, Bellvue, CO 80512. rmay@mac.com. Cartoon #63261. Used with permission.

The cartoon in chapter 12 is © 1987 by Artemas Cole. Used with permission. All rights reserved.

The cartoon in chapter 15 is © 1989 by Wendell Simons. Used with permission.

If you have comments, questions, or additional ideas,
please email the author at: kmiller@mailcti.com

Notes

How to Use This Book

1. Fred put forth a similar hope in his book *Learning to Lead: Bringing Out the Best in Others* (Waco, Tex.: Leadership/Word, 1986). To order, go to http://www.BreakfastwithFred.com.

chapter 1. What We're Up Against

1. This list was inspired by or adapted from the following: Melinda Davis, *The New Culture of Desire: Five Radical New Strategies That Will Change Your Business and Your Life* (New York: Free Press, 2002), 68–69; Lynn Lively, *Managing Information Overload* (New York: AMACOM, 1996), 3–4; and Richard Saul Wurman, *Information Anxiety* (New York: Doubleday, 1989), inside dust-jacket flap.

2. Jim Berkley, email to author, 24 April 2003.

3. Richard Saul Wurman, "Redesign the Data Dump: As the Author of 1989's *Information Anxiety* Proves Again, 'Information Architecture' Still Has a Long Way to Go," *Business 2.0*, 28 November 2000, 214.

4. Davis, *New Culture of Desire*, 54, citing a 2000 study from the University of California at Berkeley's School of Information Management and Systems.

5. Peter Large, *The Micro Revolution Revisited*, cited in Wurman, *Information Anxiety*, 35.

6. Wurman, *Information Anxiety*, 32.

7. Douglas Rushkoff, *Playing the Future: What We Can Learn from Digital Kids* (New York: Riverhead, 1996), 5.

8. Davis, *New Culture of Desire*, 28–29.

9. David Brooks, "Time to Do Everything Except Think," *Newsweek*, 30 April 2001, http://www.msnbc.com/news/562420.asp.

10. Dave Barry, "The Unbreakable Code," *Chicago Tribune Magazine*, 6 April 2003, 60.

11. Neil Postman, "Informing Ourselves to Death," (speech given at a meeting of the German Informatics Society [Gesellschaft fuer Informatik], sponsored by IBM-Germany, Stuttgart, 11 October 1990), http://world.std.com/~jimf/informing.html.

12. Wurman, *Information Anxiety*, table of contents.

13. Richard A. Swenson, M.D., *Margin: Restoring Emotional, Physical, Financial, and Time Reserves to Overloaded Lives* (Colorado Springs: NavPress, 1992), 85.

14. Patrick Kampert, "Men's Lives Are Complicated, Really," *Chicago Tribune*, 15 September 2002, sec. 2, pp. 1, 8.

15. Davis, *New Culture of Desire*, 29.

16. Ibid., 65.

17. Wurman, "Redesign the Data Dump," 211.

18. John Killinger, "Finding God in a Busy World," *Preaching Today* audio series (Carol Stream, Ill.: Christianity Today), No. 132. Available online at http://store.yahoo.com/pttranscripts/kiljohn fingod.html.

19. Bill Breen, "Desire: Connecting with What Consumers Want," *Fast Company* no. 67 (February 2003), 88. Text cited is editor Breen's summary of an interview with Melinda Davis.

20. Paul Waddington, "Dying for Information? A Report on the Effects of Information Overload in the UK and Worldwide," Reuters, United Kingdom, October 1996, cited at http://www.soft panorama.org/Social/Overload.links.shtml#Articles.

21. Jeffrey Kluger, "Too Loud, Too Bright, Too Fast," *Time*, 17 November 2002, 75, review of *Too Loud, Too Bright, Too Fast, Too Tight*, by Sharon Heller (New York: HarperCollins, 2002).

22. Ibid.

23. Craig MacInnis, email to author, 21 August 2001.

24. Wurman, "Redesign the Data Dump," 214.

chapter 2. Selecting Your Key Information Areas

1. Richard Saul Wurman, *Information Anxiety 2*, (Indianapolis: Que, 2001), 8.

2. Richard A. Swenson, M.D., *The Overload Syndrome: Learning to Live within Your Limits*, (Colorado Springs: NavPress, 1998), 136.

3. Peter F. Drucker, "Management's New Paradigms," *Forbes* (5 October 1998), http://www.forbes.com/global/1998/1005/0113052 a_print.html.

4. Smith, *Learning to Lead*, 78–79.

5. Ben Patterson, "Breadth before Depth," in "Managing the Information Overload," *Leadership* 16, no. 2 (spring 1995): 122.

6. Wurman, *Information Anxiety*, 140.

7. This phrase is from Raymond C. Ortlund, *Lord, Make My Life a Miracle* (Glendale, Calif.: Regal Books, 1974), 146.

8. Email to author, 30 June 2001.

9. T. D. Jakes, *Maximize the Moment: God's Action Plan for Your Life* (New York: Berkley, 1999), 15–16.

10. Alan Nelson, interview by author, San Diego, Calif., 28 February 2003.

11. Jay Kesler, "Filling in the Blanks," in "Managing the Information Overload," *Leadership* 16, no. 2 (spring 1995): 126.

12. David Hansen, "The Dead Writers' Society," in "Managing the Information Overload," *Leadership* 16, no. 2 (spring 1995): 125.

13. Smith, *Learning to Lead*, 85.

14. Eugene H. Peterson, *Take and Read: Spiritual Reading: An Annotated List* (Grand Rapids: Eerdmans, 1996), ix–x.

15. Parker Palmer, *Let Your Life Speak: Listening for the Voice of Vocation* (San Francisco: Jossey-Bass, 1999), 4.

chapter 3. The Fine Art of Capturing Good Ideas

1. "The For Dummies Success Story," Dummies.com, 5 May 2003, http://cda.dummies.com/WileyCDA/Section/id–100052.html.

2. John Kilcullen, in *The Marketing Revolution Newsletter*, circa 1995, published by Clement Communications, Incorporated, but now out of print.

3. Dave Goetz, email to author, 10 October 2000.

4. Anne Lamott, *Bird by Bird: Some Instructions on Writing and Life* (New York: Anchor, 1995), 133–35.

5. Tom Peters, "The Wow Project: In the New Economy, All Work Is Project Work. And You Are Your Projects! Here's How to Make Them All Go Wow!" *Fast Company* no. 24 (May 1999): 118.

6. Leith Anderson, "Curiosity Fills the Gap," in "Managing the Information Overload," *Leadership* 16, no. 2 (spring 1995): 122.

7. Lamott, *Bird by Bird*, 134.

chapter 4. How to Turn Information into Results

1. The Hope Heart Institute, "Your Health Matters," *Hope Health* newsletter, (Kalamazoo, Mich.: International Health Awareness Center, n.d.), 4. © The Hope Heart Institute, Seattle, Washington.

2. Peter F. Drucker, *The Effective Executive* (New York: Harper-Business, 1993), 5.

3. http://www.greatestquotations.com/search.asp?bedenker=Alfred+North+Whitehead&page=2.

4. Jonathan Franzen, *How to Be Alone* (New York: Farrar, Straus and Giroux, 2002), 63.

5. Craig MacInnis, email to author, 21 August 2001.

6. Sonya Yespuh, cited in Jeffrey P. Davidson, *Breathing Space: Living and Working at a Comfortable Pace in a Sped-Up Society* (New York: MasterMedia, 1991), 23.

7. Theodore Roszak, cited in Wurman, *Information Anxiety*, 32.

chapter 5. Your Information Audit

1. Helen Lee, personal correspondence, 31 March 2003.

2. William Van Winkle, "Information Overload: Fighting Data Asphyxiation Is Difficult but Possible," *Computer Bits*, http://www.computerbits.com/archive/1998/0200/infoload.html.

3. Scott Rosenberg, "Data Deluge: In the Informational Jungle, Picking Your Guide Is as Important as Keeping Your Head," *Salon*, http://archive.salon.com/april97/21st/data970410.html.

4. Anderson, "Curiosity Fills the Gap," 122.

5. Nathan Shedroff, "Forms of Information Anxiety: The Need to Be Up-to-Date and Informed Has Created a Shift to Quantity over Quality," *Business2.0*, 28 November 2000, 220.

6. Davis, *New Culture of Desire*, 56.

7. Barry Glassner, *The Culture of Fear: Why Americans Are Afraid of the Wrong Things* (New York: Basic, 1999), xxi.

8. Van Winkle, "Information Overload."

9. Barbara Brown Taylor, "People before Paper," in "Managing the Information Overload," *Leadership* 16, no. 2 (spring 1995): 124.

10. Eirik Olsen, interview by author, Wheaton, Ill., 7 January 2003.

chapter 6. How to Handle Email

1. Deborah Fallows, senior research fellow, *Email at Work*, The Pew Internet and American Life Project Survey (Washington, D.C.: Pew Internet and American Life Project, 8 December 2002): 2.

2. Categories loosely based on the "Power Emailer" definition in Fallows, *Email at Work*: 4, 17.

3. Fallows, *Email at Work*, 13.

4. Ibid., 8.

5. H. Dale Burke, "Beware 'You've Got Mail,'" *Leadership* 23, no. 4 (fall 2002): 93.

6. Fallows, *Email at Work*, 4.

7. Lisa Takeuchi Cullen, "Some More Spam, Please: Your Favorite Merchants Are Serving Tasty E-mail Offers. But Will They Get Buried in All the Trash?" *Time*, 11 November 2002, http://www.time.com/time/magazine/article/ 0,9171,1101021111– 386956,00.html.

8. Saul Hansell, "Internet Is Losing Ground in Battle against Spam," *New York Times*, 22 April 2003, http://www.nytimes.com, then search the archive. Hansell writes, "Brightmail, which makes spam-filtering software for corporate networks and big Internet providers, says that 45 percent of the e-mail it now sees is junk, up from 16 percent in January 2002. America Online says the amount of spam aimed at its 35 million customers has doubled since the beginning of this year and now approaches two billion messages a day, more than 70 percent of the total it receives."

9. Jakob Nielsen, "Information Pollution," Useit.com, 11 August 2003, http://www.useit.com/alertbox/20030811.html.

10. "E-Mail Spam: How to Stop It from Stalking You," *Consumer Reports*, August 2003, 12.

11. Doris Igna, cited in Jesse Berst, "End Inbox Blues: Common-sense Ways to Control Email Overload," *ZDNet*, 5 July 2000, http://www.zdnet.com/anchordesk/stories/story/0,10738,2597972, 00.html.

12. Paul Eng, "Taming 'Occupational Spam': Software to Help Sort the Wheat and Chaff of Work E-Mails," ABCnews.com, http://abcnews.go.com/sections/scitech/CuttingEdge/cuttingedge 020802.html.

13. Thomas A. Stewart, *The Wealth of Knowledge: Intellectual Capital and the Twenty-First Century Organization* (New York: Currency/Doubleday, 2001), 7.

14. Stanley Bing, "Log Off, You Losers! Electronic Flatulence Must Cease!" *Fortune*, 10 November 2002, http://www.fortune.com/for tune/bing/0,15704,390092,00.html.

15. "Email Change-of-Address Services Merge," EmailUniverse.com, 29 October 2001, http://emailuniverse.com/list-news/2001/10/29.html.

16. Van Winkle, "Information Overload."

17. Bing, "Log Off, You Losers!"

18. Berst, "End Inbox Blues."

19. Charles Henderson, "No More Medical Roulette: Publisher Says Internet Will Change in 2003," 12 January 2003, http://www.NewsRx.com.

20. Jakob Nielsen, "Email Newsletters Pick Up Where Websites Leave Off," Jakob Nielsen's Alertbox, 30 September 2002, http://www.useit.com/alertbox/20020930.html.

21. Fallows, Email at Work.

22. "E-Mail Spam," 12.

23. Eng, "Taming 'Occupational Spam.'"

24. John Markoff, "Start-Up Aims to End Spam," New York Times, 24 March 2003, http://www.nytimes.com/2003/03/24/technology/24PHIL.html.

25. "E-Mail Spam," 13.

26. Ibid., 15.

27. Mark Board, "Going Upstream to Fight Spam," Wired News, http://www.wired.com/news/infostructure/0,1377,61971,00.html.

28. Rich Tatum, email to author, 19 March 2003.

29. Fallows, Email at Work, 12, citing Stephanie Olsen, "Spam flood forces companies to take desperate measures," CNET News.com, 21 March 2002. http://news.com.com/2009-1023-864815.html.

chapter 7. How to Find What You Need Online

1. Wurman, "Redesign the Data Dump," 212.

2. Geoffrey Nunberg, "As Google Goes, So Goes the Nation," New York Times, 18 May 2003, http://wwww.nytimes.com, http://www-csli.stanford.edu/~nunberg/google.html. The percentage is variously reported. Lev Grossman, in "Search and Destroy" (Time, 22 December 2003), writes, "Right now 32% of all Web searches go through google.com. That number shoots to around 70% when you count searches on sites like AOL.com, which licenses Google's technology."

3. Janet Rubenking, "Search Smarter," *PC*, 4 February 2003, 66–67.

4. Richard Saul Wurman, "Warp-Speed Rules: What Successful Designers and Communicators Need to Master in a Net-Connected World," *Business 2.0*, 28 November 2000, 222.

chapter 8. How to Handle Voice Mail, Junk Mail, and Magazines

1. Eric W. Weisstein, "The Trouble with Tribbles," Eric's Excruciatingly Detailed Star Trek (TOS) Plot Summaries, http://www.ericweisstein.com/fun/startrek/TheTroubleWithTribbles.html.

2. Richard A. Swenson, M.D., *The Overload Syndrome* (Colorado Springs: NavPress, 1998), 138.

3. Ibid., 142.

4. Ibid., 140.

5. Maxie Dunnam, Gordon MacDonald, and Donald W. McCullough, *Mastering Personal Growth* (Sisters, Ore.: Multnomah, 1992), 103.

6. Privacy Rights Clearinghouse, "Fact Sheet 4: Reducing Junk Mail," http://www.privacyrights.org/fs/fs4-junk.htm.

7. Ibid.

8. Center for a New American Dream, "Declaring Your Independence from Junk Mail: A How-To Guide," http://www.newdream.org/junkmail/optout.html.

9. National Waste Prevention Coalition, "Business Junk Mail Reduction Project," 17 July 2002, http://dnr.metrokc.gov/swd/nwpc/bizjunkmail.htm.

10. Ibid.

11. Richard Carlson, *Don't Sweat the Small Stuff at Work: Simple Ways to Minimize Stress and Conflict while Bringing Out the Best in Yourself and Others* (New York: Hyperion, 1998), 17.

12. Tamara Foreman, email to author, 7 April 2003.

13. Quentin Schultze, "Practical Disciplines to Live Well in the Midst of Intrusive Communications Technology," interviewed by Ken Myers, *Mars Hill Audio Journal* 59 (November/December 2002).

14. "'Do-Not-Call' Still a Big Hit," CBSNews.com, http://www.cbsnews.com/stories/2003/03/11/politics/main543573.shtml.

15. James D. Berkley, email to author, 24 April 2003.

16. Smith, *Learning to Lead*, 80.

chapter 9. How to Organize, File, and Store Information

1. John Ortberg, "Diagnosing Hurry Sickness: How Do You Know If You Suffer from Hurry Sickness?" *Leadership* 19, no. 4 (fall 1998), http://www.christianitytoday.com/le/8l4/8l4031.html.

2. David Shenk, *Data Smog: Surviving the Information Glut*, revised and expanded (San Francisco: HarperSanFrancisco, 1998), 30, cited in Swenson, *Overload Syndrome*, 138.

3. Lisa Skolnik, "Buried Alive," *Chicago Tribune*, 6 November 2002, sec. 6, pp. 1, 4.

4. Smith, *Learning to Lead*, 86–87.

5. Harriet Schlechter, cited in Lisa Skolnik, "Purge the Piles," *Chicago Tribune*, 6 November 2002, sec. 6, p. 1.

6. Ibid.

7. Ibid.

8. Fred Smith, *Learning to Lead*, 64.

9. Stephanie Winston, *The Organized Executive: New Ways to Manage Time, Paper, People, and the Electronic Office; Updated and Revised for the Nineties* (New York: Norton, 1994), 42–45, 64.

chapter 10. Tap the Power of Block Days

1. Bill Hoyt, email to author, 20 December 2000. Bill is executive director of NexStep Coaching, http://www.nexstepcoaching.org.

2. Smith, *Learning to Lead*, 89–90.

3. Swenson, *Overload Syndrome*, 59.

4. Carlson, *Don't Sweat the Small Stuff at Work*, 208.

5. Drucker, "Time Management," 75.

6. Eirik Olsen, email to author, 11 January 2003.

7. Swenson, *Overload Syndrome*, 62.

8. John C. Maxwell, *Thinking for a Change: Eleven Ways Highly Successful People Approach Life and Work* (New York: Warner, 2002), 39.

9. H. Dale Burke, "How to Overcome Overload: You Can't Keep Your Act Together unless You Learn to Balance All the 'Stuff' of Ministry," *Leadership* 19, no. 4 (fall 2002), http://www.christianity today.com/le/2002/004/14.90.html.

10. Dunnam, MacDonald, and McCullough, *Mastering Personal Growth*, 99.

11. Stephen Franklin, "Cogs in the Machine: Running Faster Just to Fall Further Behind," *Chicago Tribune*, 15 September 2002, http://personal.monm.edu/jkessler/Art-Running-Faster-Fall-Behind.htm.

chapter 11. Try an Info-Techno Sabbath

1. Exodus 31:12–13, 15 (NLT).
2. Hilton Generational Time Survey of 1,220 adults in January 2001, cited in "Overworked Americans," www.PreachingToday.com.
3. Ken Myers, "Drowning in Information," *Tabletalk*, November 2000, 14. *Tabletalk* may be ordered from Ligonier Ministries, http://www.gospelcom.net/ligonier/.
4. George Gilder, cited in Swenson, *Overload Syndrome*, 148.
5. Neil Postman, *The End of Education: Redefining the Value of School* (New York: Alfred A. Knopf, 1995), 38.
6. John Ortberg, "Choosing a Slower Lane," www.christianitytoday.com/leaders/newsletter/2002/cln20711.html.
7. Smith, *Learning to Lead*, 77–78.
8. Wurman, "Redesign the Data Dump," 214, 216.
9. Hugh Heclo, commenting on the results of the excesses of technology, cited in David Shenk, *Data Smog: Surviving the Information Glut*, revised and expanded (San Francisco: HarperSanFrancisco, 1998), 199.
10. Richard Winter, interview by Todd Hertz, "Is God Exciting Enough? The Author of *Still Bored in a Culture of Entertainment* Says That Increased Stimulation Has Caused a 'Deadness of Soul.' What Can Turn It Around?" *Christianity Today*, 15 January 2003, http://www.christianitytoday.com/ct/2003/102/31.0.html.
11. Swenson, *Overload Syndrome*, 51.
12. Mary Ann Jeffreys, comp., "Colorful Sayings of Colorful Luther," *Christian History* 11, no. 2 (issue 34, 1992): 28.
13. François Fénelon, *The Seeking Heart* (Sargent, Ga.: Christian Books Publishing House, 1992), 110, 97.
14. Davis, *New Culture of Desire*, 58.
15. Annie Dillard, *Teaching a Stone to Talk: Expeditions and Encounters* (New York: HarperCollins, 1998), 31.

chapter 12. Why We Secretly Like Overload

1. Brooks, "Time to Do Everything Except Think."
2. Van Winkle, "Information Overload."

3. Marcus Buckingham and Donald O. Clifton, *Now, Discover Your Strengths* (New York: Free Press, 2001), http://www.Strengths Finder.com.

4. Fallows, *Email at Work*, 16.

5. Email to author, May 2001.

6. These questions are inspired by Smith, *Learning to Lead*, 77.

7. Statistics from Robert D. Putnam, *Bowling Alone: The Collapse and Revival of American Community* (New York: Simon and Schuster, 2000), cited in "No Time for Relationships," www.Preaching Today.com.

8. Bill Hybels, *Courageous Leadership* (Grand Rapids: Zondervan, 2002). This excerpt appeared as "The Art of Self-Leadership," *Leadership* 22, no. 3 (summer 2001), http://www.christianitytoday.com/bcl/areas/vision-strategy/articles/le–2001–003–13.86.html.

9. Helen Lee, email to author, 1 April 2002.

10. Smith, *Learning to Lead*, 64–65.

11. Shedroff, "Forms of Information Anxiety," 220.

12. Ibid.

13. Patterson, "Breadth before Depth," 122.

14. Fénelon, *The Seeking Heart*, 62.

15. "Deepening Our Conversation with God: A Classic *Leadership* Interview with Henri Nouwen and Richard Foster," *Leadership* 18, no. 1 (winter 1997), http://www.christianitytoday.com/bcl/areas/spiritualgrowth/articles/le–711–71112a.html.

16. Romans 8:38–39, my paraphrase.

17. Email to author, May 2001.

18. Sir Alec Paterson, cited in *Leadership* 1, no. 2 (spring 1980), http://www.preachingtoday.com/index.taf?_UserReference=F7A47 5DF836CC7F53EFDD6B7&_function=illustration&_op=show_norm&IID=1399&sr=1.

chapter 13. Blessed Are They Who Admit Their Ignorance . . .

1. Wurman, *Information Anxiety*, 53.

2. Swenson, *Overload Syndrome*, 141.

3. Ikujiro Nonaka, "The Knowledge-Creating Company," in *Harvard Business Review on Knowledge Management* (Boston: Harvard Business Review Press, 1998), 26–27.

4. Maxwell, *Thinking for a Change*, 44.

5. Swenson, *Margin*, 83.

6. Thomas de Zengotita, "The Numbing of the American Mind: Culture as Anesthetic," *Harper's*, April 2002, 35.

7. Melinda Davis, cited in Breen, "Desire: Connecting with What Consumers Want," 89.

8. George W. S. Trow, *Within the Context of No Context* (Boston: Atlantic Monthly Press, 1997), cited in Rosenberg, "Data Deluge."

9. Winter, interview, "Is God Exciting Enough?"

10. Todd Gitlin, "How the Torrent of Images and Sounds Overwhelms Our Lives," interview by Ken Myers, *Mars Hill Audio Journal* 59 (November/December 2002).

11. Ted Baehr, cited in Swenson, *Overload Syndrome*, 146.

12. Winter, interview, "Is God Exciting Enough?"

13. Eric Reed, "Chocolate? No, TV: Our Unusual Lenten Fast," *Leadership Weekly* email newsletter, 4 April 2001, http://www.christianitytoday.com/leaders/newsletter/2001/cln10404.html.

14. Barbara Brown Taylor, "People before Paper," in "Managing the Information Overload," *Leadership* 16, no. 2, (spring 1995): 124.

15. Dave Goetz, "Suburban Spirituality: The Land of SUVs and Soccer Leagues Tends to Weather the Soul in Peculiar Ways, but It Doesn't Have To," *Christianity Today*, July 2003, 35–36.

16. Theodore Roszak, *The Cult of Information: The Folklore of Computers and the True Art of Thinking* (New York: Pantheon, 1986), 92.

17. Ibid.

18. Shedroff, "Forms of Information Anxiety," 220.

19. Postman, "Informing Ourselves to Death."

20. Wurman, "Redesign the Data Dump," 220.

21. Lee Eclov, email to author, March 2003.

chapter 14. Great Information on Information

1. Smith, *Learning to Lead*, 65–66.

2. Swenson, *Overload Syndrome*, 135.

chapter 15. A Word for Church Leaders

1. John R. W. Stott, *Between Two Worlds: The Challenge of Preaching Today* (Grand Rapids: Eerdmans, 1994), n.p.

2. Smith, *Learning to Lead*, 73.

3. Richard Kriegbaum, in *Leadership Prayers* (Carol Stream, Ill.: Tyndale, 1998), 14–15.

Index

Boldface page numbers indicate illustrations. Page numbers followed by *t* indicate tables and graphs.

Kevin A. Miller is vice president of resources for Christianity Today International, editor-at-large of *Leadership* journal, and executive editor for PreachingToday.com. He is the author of numerous periodical articles as well as the books *Secrets of Staying Power* and *More Than You and Me.*